LETTER TO THE 8 YEAR OLD ME

BY

LATONYA PEROSSIER

The life you think you see sometimes is the life we want you to see. I have been on this earth long enough to know that then you walk in your truth your truth is all you have. I love the person I have become even though it took me a lifetime.

CONTENTS

CHAPTER 1: The Conversation

CHAPTER 2: How Could this Happen

CHAPTER 3: Letter to my Family

CHAPTER 4: Letter to my Predator

CHAPTER 5: Letter to my Friends

CHAPTER 6: Letter to my Sons

CHAPTER 7: Letter to the **48** Year Old Me

CHAPTER 8: Letter to the **8** Year Old Me

LETTER TO THE 8 YEAR OLD ME

"If you're going through hell, keep going."
Winston Churchill

THE CONVERSATION

In every situation, you must understand how you got there. Well, I understand how I got to this moment. I was 8 and my life changed forever. I never got over what happened to me at that time, and it has affected every aspect of my life. This book started from a conversation with a good friend of mine. I needed a break from work, and we hadn't seen one another in a while. I had a free stay at a hotel, and we thought it would be a great idea to meet and catch up with one another. My friend said to me that she was going to figure me out that weekend because I had been doing and saying some strange things and she felt they needed to be addressed. She's a little pushy but you got to love her, she really means well. I cried a lot of tears that weekend, but I had a good friend that wanted me to heal. While sitting on the bed and through my tears I told her that the 8yr old me was still hurt and I didn't know how to heal her. She deserves to be whole. She deserves to know that what happened to her was not her fault and she was not old enough to understand she was not to blame. Now, when you think of a 48yr old woman referring to her 8yr old self you must believe that it must have been a doozy. Yes, it was, and this book is a healing of the soul for me. I need to forgive myself and all the people I felt didn't do their part in keeping me safe and the people that hurt me. I have always known that I wanted to do this but there is a part of me that is embarrassed about the story I must tell. I know that I shouldn't be because I was a kid, a child and I had no control over what happened to me. So, for years I have held this story close to my heart because it always broke my heart. The sad part is sometimes I felt like I deserved to have a broken heart. Not sure why I felt that way, but I was struggling with the truth that I held so long, and it had created in me a sense of guilt that I was not sure I wanted to let go. It had been a part of me for so long. When the "me too" movement came out I cried for days. Not because I was sad for the women, but because I was one of those women and I didn't have the strength to say anything. I wanted to post "me too" but I was too embarrassed to do so. Can you believe a grown woman ashamed to speak her truth? In one weekend with a really close friend and a lot of tears I decided to release all my hurt and pain with a letter to my 8yr old self. This letter is a healing of my soul that I hope brings me out of the desperation I have lived in most of my life. Do I know for sure that this letter is going to work? No, I don't, but I have decided that I'm going to give it a try. I need for her to know that I love her, and she is not broken and is worthy of love. I have been going to counseling because I know I need help and I thought counseling would give me that help. I can't lie it's good to talk to someone who has no investment in me. I can tell them all the things I'm feeling about myself, my life and the people that affect it. Having a conversation about my childhood is always hard because the memories are filled with pain. At one point in my life, I would not talk about it with anyone because I was really embarrassed and thought no one should know anything about this. Who knows this may not heal me, but it may heal someone else struggling with the deep secret of molestation and rape! I am far from an expert, and I don't know what I'm doing at all. I am a woman telling a story of my life and hoping at the end I can walk away with a peace that surpasses all understanding. I really don't know what that peace looks like, but I can assure you it has to be better than were I am now. My counselor told me to tell my husband of my tragedy and a part of me immediately sunk in my chair. I was afraid he would see me differently. That broken little girl that I look at everyday in the mirror and try to wipe away with perfect hair and makeup. That girl who remembers every detail of every assault and hates that she can remember them. That little girl that feels a certain kind of way when she sees a man interact with a little girl because in her eyes, he is going to hurt her like I was hurt. That little girl! In the last chapter of this book, I'm going to formally introduce you to her, and I hope that you cannot relate to her but can feel for her. My husband was awesome he wanted to take my pain away by any means necessary, but like anything in the past you can only reflect, learn, and heal. I'm ready to grow her up; she deserves to be an adult.

LETTER TO THE 8 YEAR OLD ME

"Turn your wounds into wisdom" Oprah Winfrey

HOW COULD THIS HAPPEN

I was born September 6, 1972, five miles south of the post office in Pineville, LA. according to my original birth certificate. Which also stated I was a negro girl born to a negro mother and father. The story from my mother was, she was on the stretcher and the doctor told her not to push. "Well, I was in a lot of pain" my mother said so she pushed me out on the stretcher. Growing up in Bunkie, LA. I really don't remember much at all. I moved to Houston, TX. at a very young age. We moved to Texas because my mom was leaving my father and coming to live with my grandmother until she got on her feet. My mother was raised by her aunt but somehow, my mother and my grandmother developed a relationship. Now, we were not a small family by no stretch of the imagination. It was Brad, my brothers Josh who we call Jun, Gene, Jay, Carl, Rod, sisters Tessa, Londa, and myself. On top of that my mother had taken custody of two of my cousins, because their parents had passed away. Jo and Anna had other siblings, but my mother took them two. My sister Londa and I were the youngest of all my brothers and sisters. I was 8yrs younger than my youngest brother, my sister was 3yrs younger than me. My sister and myself are the last two born and we both have different fathers. On the way from Louisiana the U-Haul turned over and we lost everything. So, at a very young age I was learning to deal with loss, and it was only going to get worse. After living with my grandmother for a very short while my mother got a place in 5th Ward. I remember my father had made his way back into our lives and he and my mother were sitting on the porch, and I was showing them my dance moves. A boy from the neighborhood came up behind me and grabbed my waist. I turned and said to him in my clearest best voice, "uh oh you then done it now, I'm going to kick your ass!" That came out of my mouth before I could even think that I probably shouldn't say it. Both of my parents' mouth flew open and I knew immediately I was in a great deal of trouble. My mother turned to my father and stated, "You better get her because if I do, I'm going to kill her!" My father told me to come in the house because he was going to beat my butt! When I got inside, he laid me across his knee whispered in my ear when I spank you, you better cry because if not your mother is going to get you. My father spanked me, and I cried with real tears because I was so hurt that my dad hit me. As a young girl my dad was everything to me, I adored him. He was barely around as I got older, but I still loved him more than anything. After leaving 5th Ward my family, which consisted of my mother, my baby sister and myself moved to 3rd Ward. My other brothers and sisters were out of the house and living on their own. Some moved to 3rd Ward to be near us, and others stayed in 5th Ward. We moved into this apartment complex that was not much of nothing, but my mom could work there as the building manager and we could live there for free, we were poor, and I knew it. But I was a kid and I learned at an early age how to make do. My mother received food stamps and public assistance for us and that kept food on the table. When I got old enough my mother would send me to the grocery store with food stamps to buy food, I was so embarrassed! Not sure why because at least they kept food on the table. Yet, I hated when my mom asked me to go to the store with them. By the age of 12 I had started my own business because even though we were poor I really was into fashion. I knew what I wanted to wear even though I couldn't afford it. My business was a cleaning service and if I didn't know anything I knew how to clean. My mother would make us get up every Saturday and we had to clean the house from the top to the bottom. I would also start dinner for you if you wanted. I would charge $20 to clean your house and start dinner. I made flyers with crayons that said I was a cleaning service for hire. I loved fashion so, I would look in magazines and watch fashion on TV and would say one day I was going to be able to afford to wear the things I like. I was 12, when I started my business cleaning resident's apartments in my building. I would use that money to buy the clothes and shoes that I wanted. Once I started working, I never stopped. I always had some kind of job; it was either after school or a summer job. At the age of 13 my mother put me in etiquette classes. Where I learned dinning, sitting, and great posture etiquette. I had also competed in my first pageant, The Miss America Coed Pageant. No, I did not win but that is when I realized that I wanted to be successful in life and not be the girl that didn't measure up to anybody in the room. I knew I wanted to be a force to recon with. In high school I always felt as if I didn't measure up. Yes, I was a cheerleader, ran track, was on the swim team, played basketball and was the president of student council, but still felt like I didn't measure up. My friends all had things that I wanted, and that always made me feel like I was less than. My friends were great to me, they would let me borrow clothing and things, so that I could fit in, but I really didn't. I had always wanted to be a writer when I was in school and one of my teachers really believed in me. He would always tell me that I would be a great writer one day. I would write a few things over the years, mostly poetry but I started the first time trying to write a book about 20yrs ago. I was not ready to really talk about the things that broke my heart at that time, it was too hard. When I was a Senior in High School we had a gentleman by the name, Montel Williams come to the school, and he addressed the Senior class. He was in this white uniform, and he talked about making great decisions and such, but he said something so profound that it changed my life. He said, "You can be anything you want to be as long as you believe it!" Being from the hood you don't hear things like that. I believed it, and I was going to do everything in my power to do whatever it was I thought I could do. I joined the Navy at the age of 20 and I can tell you that was the best thing I could have ever done. I really believe that if I had stayed in Houston, I would have been just another statistic. I modeled a little while living in Virginia. I modeled for Keith Sweat's sister; funny I can't even remember her name. I guess that is how life goes. If a person doesn't make an impact in your life you forget about them. She is how I got to meet Keith Sweat many years ago. I even got to hang out at his home, which was absolutely beautiful. He was a very gracious person, and I had a wonderful time hanging out in his studio. Since being in the Navy I have met some pretty interesting people and have had a lot of fun. The Navy definitely changed my life for the better. I would always try and sneak home and surprise my family for birthdays. I felt as if I was so far removed from my family that I tried everything to keep some kind of connection to them. I never wanted to lose my family to the Navy, even though sometimes I felt I did. I missed so many things being in the Navy, but I will never say that I wish I never did it. My father died on my 21st birthday when I was stationed in Norfolk, VA. Now, as I stated before my father was everything to me, but he was also an abuser. Never to me but my mother received the wrath of my father on a regular basis.

Fortunately, I don't have any memories of his abuse, but my brothers and sisters spoke of it often. The one story that sticks out to me was the time my father didn't want my mother to go to church and she went anyway! My brother told me that my father was sitting in the house with his shot gun waiting on my mother to return. As soon as she walked through the door, he was going to blow her away. My brother took off running down the street to warn my mother not to come home that day because of the danger that was waiting for her. I never really understood why my mother left my father and moved to Texas, because I never witnessed or remember any fighting but when I got older, and my brother told me that story I completely understood. I went home for his funeral and grieved for the man that I loved dearly. We all loved him he was our father, but he was not a great example of what kind of husband to be. Now, if you wanted to know what a man looked like that took care of his responsibilities, that was my father. I believe that everything has a cause and effect so, let me tell you how this started. I started getting molested from age 8 to about 13 years old. Sitting here trying to remember the first time it happened is very sad to me, because that means I have suppressed it so deep that I almost don't want to remember. So, the first time it happened at 8 was with a stranger. If I saw this man, I would not know him. My aunt Janice used to have an apartment in the same complex as us and she would have all these strangers at her house. Let me give you a little background on my aunt before I continue. My aunt was a semiprofessional pool player. She played all over Houston and Louisiana from what I remember when I was a very young girl. She taught me how to play pool at a very young age and I got pretty good at it. Nowhere close to her level of playing but I was a very decent player. My aunt is also a lesbian and has been one all my life. I have never known or seen her with the opposite sex. I admired her so much as a kid. She seemed to have her life together and was living a good life. I would go over to her apartment all the time so that she could give me pool playing lessons. This one particular day I went to her house, and she had friends over. I came in and she was mingling with her friends. I told her I had come for my lesson, but she was a little busy. I thought I would just hang around until she was done then I could get my lesson. There was a man there that walked over to me immediately and started talking to me. I'm 8 so I just start talking to him. Of course, I can't remember what the conversation was about, but he took me by the hand and took me in one of the rooms. To be honest I really don't know what was going through my head. I didn't understand what was happening. He undressed me and started to touch me in my private area. He told me this is what people do when they like one another. I was confused because I didn't know him well enough to like him. He laid me down on a blanket he put on the floor and got on top of me. I told him it hurt he said,

"It's ok I'm not going to put it all the way in." Now, you are probably wondering how I remember that. It is etched in my mind. I have never forgotten that part and I never will. I laid there while this grown man molested me on the floor of my aunt's apartment. I don't know why I didn't scream or cry out. I have thought about that a lot lately because a part of me feels like I didn't because I liked it. How could I just let this stranger do that to me and not cry out or try to stop him? If you judge me, it's ok because I judge myself every day. When he was done, he put my clothes back on and I went home. I never told anyone and to this day that bothers me. I was an innocent little girl, and that innocence was taken from me. At that moment the course of my life was changed, and I hear people say that things happen for a reason. Why would this happen to an innocent little girl? The unfortunate part is that is not the end of this story, it only gets worse, and I have the scares to prove it. As I said before, I never reported this to anyone and I as an 8yr old picked up the pieces and moved on. So, when I was at my godparents' house one day and my godfather Ratcliff grabbed my breast, I thought I must be doing something to make these people do these things to me. His wife left him there with me to go to the store. Why would she think anything like that would happen? Or maybe she knew what he wanted to do and left so that he could molest and rape a little girl. When she left, he took my bottoms off and put his mouth on me and put his fingers inside me. He again said, "This is what people do when they like one another!" I loved my godfather, so I didn't question his actions. I was just confused at how you show love to people. I was not an adult, but I knew what we were doing was what adults did. I really don't know how I knew that, but I did. It hurt and I was not happy at all about what was taking place with me. My godfather was touching me as much as he could. I tried my best to stay away but his wife was always asking my mom to send me over because she has some things for me to do to make some money. As I had stated earlier, I had started my own business and I was doing really well because people in my apartment complex wanted someone else to clean their place. We didn't have a lot and I was getting ready for middle school, and I was not going to start middle school with clothes from Goodwill. So, that summer I worked extra hard, and I made enough money to buy my school clothes for that year without the help of my mom and I was proud of myself. Under being proud of myself I felt dirty. When I found out my godfather had passed away many years later, my only thought was now you're in the eternal hell that you deserve. One of my other clients was my uncle by marriage, I guess. My brothers and sisters called him uncle, so I guess he was. My uncle Zet was the family member that got drunk and talked loudly and made a scene. He knew I had started my business and he wanted me to come over to clean and start dinner for him on occasion. His wife Lauran my aunt as I knew her had passed away and he now lived alone. I can remember when I went over the first time to clean and start dinner it was easy. We talked about what I was doing in school and my friends as I cleaned the bathroom then the bedroom and when I got to the living room, he grabbed me and pulled me down on the couch on top of him. It had happened so often that I had become accustomed to being molested and raped. I stopped feeling bad for myself and started thinking I deserved it in some crazy way. By this time, I was 12 and I was well versed in the activity that we call adulting. As he raped me there on the couch, I just thought what my aunt would think of her husband doing the things he was doing to me. I knew I hated it, but I didn't stop him, and I don't know why I never stopped any of them. I fight myself everyday about that because how could I not say to someone that I was being touched and handled inappropriately by adults. My uncle was inappropriate with me for about a year, and I hated him so much! In fact, when he passed away my family asked if I would come home for the funeral. The only reason I came home was to see him in that casket and thank God for taking him away and praying that he lives an eternal hell! I know that sounds horrible and mean, and if you are a Christian, you're thinking that is not very Christian like. I get it I am supposed to forgive people for the wrong that they do because it's what God has taught us to do. I'm going to say this. I am a Christian and now I forgive him but back then when

I was a 29-year-old young woman struggling to figure out where she belonged in this world, I hated him, and I was happy he had a hard life after I left for the Navy. It wasn't just him that I hated, I hated all the men that took a part of that 8-year-old little girl who grew up struggling to figure it out. The worst one was someone that I loved dearly. I was 8yrs old and I remember this one because it was the most devastating one. I was sleeping and I felt something hurting my private area and it made me wake up. I was confused to see who this was, and I was not sure why this was happening to me. At 8 your mind is so fragile and innocent that you really don't know what or why this is happening. I do remember thinking this does not feel right. I also remember wanting him to stop that. The only thing I could muster out of my mouth at that time was, "It hurts!" He stopped and never did that again. Unfortunately for me the damage had been done and I became the 8-year-old that would be raped and molested for several years to come. I often wonder if it changed my inside to reflect on the outside. Did I deserve it? What I know for sure is that it made me a vulnerable little girl. Vulnerable to the prey of men who had malice in their heart and disregard for a little girl trying to make it in the world. I was that little girl that was hurt over and over again and then I became that women that was hurt over and over again. I know you are wondering why I won't reveal who the beginner of this tragedy is, I'm not ready and I don't think that I ever will be. I have lived with that for 40yrs, and I think it's ok to go another. If I ever did that, I would destroy myself and I will not do that. It will not give me any closure there is no such thing in this instance. This is the very first time I have ever written those words. I only write them to be honest with myself and in hopes to heal myself. It hurt a long time and I can no longer hurt. Yes, I was devastated to see who it was and at that time I did not know what was happening should not have been happening. I watch TV and I see these shows of women confronting their abusers and taking back what they took from them, and I feel shame because I could not be that brave. In some ways I am a coward. I never said anything, and I never confronted them. Yes, I know I was a kid, but that kid became an adult, and that adult didn't do anything to rescue that kid. So, that kid has been sitting in a corner trying in vain to heal herself. So, I did things that were familiar to me. I became promiscuous because that is what I knew. I secretly hated men and wanted to destroy them because they were the enemy. I learned to manipulate them because I knew what they wanted I found that out at 8yrs old. I used that to my advantage, and it made me feel powerful. What I didn't realize was that is what made me weak. That is what made me vulnerable to predators and I was always the prey. At one point I got tired, and I wanted to get myself together because I knew I deserved better. I didn't date for a long time and all I wanted to do was work on me. I did it, I coached myself through being a woman and knowing my worth because I didn't know. I thought I was great because men found me attractive and that was what I needed. See, a part of me felt so unattractive as a young girl because I felt so ugly inside and it spilled over to the outside of me. When I looked in the mirror, I didn't see the beautiful young woman that I should have seen. I saw the little girl that had been raped and molested and that was ugly to me. If people knew that truth, I would be ugly to them too. I remember distinctively when I felt like I was an attractive woman. I was 26yrs old and I had been married a few years. I already had two children and spent a year going through postpartum depression. Then one day like a light it just switched on. I looked in the mirror and I didn't see a wounded little girl I saw a beautiful woman that was going to make them all pay. Pay for all the damage that had been caused to me. Pay they did so, I thought. It's strange looking back on that and seeing the truth in those moments now. I was a wounded little girl crying for help and I didn't know how to help her. I just kept piling things on her and hoping she would just go away. I hope this heals her because I'm all out of options. I joined the Navy over 29 years ago and I can say that it was one of the best decisions I had made. I was given resources that could help me recover and grow. I can remember one time the Navy sent me to anger management classes. Yes, I was angry because that little girl was fighting me to come out and I would not let her. I went to those classes, and they just taught me how to cope with my anger not to heal. That was ok for the time being because I just wanted it to stop being so hard to deal with men. I felt that a lot of the time when they would reprimand me it wasn't because I had actually done something, it was because they were attracted to me and punishing me was their way of controlling the situation. As strange as that might seem, I feel there is some truth to it. I really don't care what anyone else thinks this is my truth. As I said before I'm no expert and I don't proclaim to be. I'm writing my truth in hopes to walk away free of my shackle that has been pinning me down for 40 years now. Even in writing this I feel an overwhelming fear of rejection and judgement. I know not everyone is going to like what I have to say. With every stroke of this keyboard, I feel weaker but stronger. I will finish this, and, in the end, I hope to cry harder than I have ever cried before, then walk away whole. With a peace no one can take away from me because I have earned it. I don't think you can understand never in your 40 years feeling real peace!

LETTER TO THE 8 YEAR OLD ME

"Other things may change us, but we start and end with the family" Anthony Brandt

LETTER TO MY FAMILY

First, I would have to say, I blamed you for everything that happened to me. I felt like you all didn't protect me from the monsters of the world. I start my letter to you in this way because I had so much hurt in me from my family that I loved you differently for a very long time. I loved you guys, but I also had a dislike that I fought a long time to peel off. Where were you when I was getting dealt with like an adult at 8yrs old? How could you not see the signs of a child crying out for help, are the questions I asked myself over and over again. Now, that I got that off my chest let's talk! My family was a pretty large one. My brothers and sisters were all pretty much grown by the time I was 8yrs old and mostly on their own. We all still lived near one another, no one was ever too far away from one another. My mother did everything she could do to make sure my younger sister and I had what we needed, but let's face it my mother had us late in the game and I'm sure she was tired. Coming up in the 80's my family dealt with the same things most Black families dealt with during that time. Poverty, racism, unemployment, and crime were the leading obstacles of people of color during that time. Like most Black people we figured out how to make it work. Unfortunately, not all of it was legal. Some of my sibling chose to make their money illegally and others got a job and did the right thing. I'm not saying that to talk bad about my family, I'm being transparent. They did what they had to do to survive. This is a letter of reflection and forgiveness. If you are judging anything that is said in this book it's not for you. During the time of me being raped and molested my brothers and sisters lived around us some in the same apartment complex, but did not live in the house with my mom, my sister, and I. Even though we lived in separate homes it didn't feel that way because we were always at one another's house for some reason or another. I can say this about us we always found a reason to have a get-together. So, before I get into my siblings let me tell you a little bit about my mother. My mother got married to my father at the of 17 I think, and they immediately started having children. My mother in total had nine children and adopted two of our cousins. My mother is from Louisiana and had to pick cotton at a point in her life. My mother told me that when she was in school, girls where not allow to learn math, they had to learn cooking and sewing. As I stated earlier my mother was raised by her aunt because my grandmother left her at the hospital. Now, the story goes that my mother was too dark, that is why she was left at the hospital. This is real life shit that black folks lived back then. So, my mother was the best mother you could ever meet. She knew what it felt like to be unwanted, and she made sure that none of us ever felt that feeling. Now, if she needed to kick your ass, she was willing and able. She would always tell us to do the right thing even though sometimes we did not do it. My mother had a stroke giving birth to my little sister and it paralyzed her on the left side. So, she had very little use of her left hand which had paralysis. That never stopped her from doing anything she needed to do. This is why my mother is my superhero. I saw this woman make things happen even with her limitations. My mother was considered disabled due to the stroke and everything that happened because of it. So, we lived in a low-income area, but my mother made sure that we always had food on the table, and we looked nice. When my sister and I were young my mother would let us play dress up in her clothes. One night my sister and I were playing with our dolls and playing dress up. I placed my doll on the heater because her hair needed to dry. While the family was sleeping my doll caught on fire. My brother woke us all up to get out of the house. Me and my sister was still in my mom's clothes that we had been playing in earlier. So, my brother picked us up and placed us out the window to safety. A crowd had formed because the fire was in our apartment and people are just nosey. My mom was getting out of the window, so she put one leg out. For whatever reason she thought she was tall. My mom is five feet one-inch-tall lady so, when she leaned over to bring the other leg out, she flipped out the window. Her dress went over her head, and she was on the ground. My sister and I ran over to get her up. Once we got everything under control, meaning the fire was out and we could go back into the house, we laughed so hard and so did my mom. I know if my mom knew what was happening to me, she would have not stopped until she got them all, but I never told her because I didn't want to hurt her. I didn't want her to feel like she failed me as my mom. She had enough trauma to deal with and I didn't want to add to it. My mom has dementia now, and I am so sad because the women that was so sharp all my life is now not remembering the simple things. The reason why dementia is so sad is because they eventually forget who they are and who the people that love them are. They spend the remainder of their lives with people reminding them who they are and who they are to them. The sad part is all the grandkids that she damn near raised don't even come around to see her, even if it's just so she can see their faces. These will be the same people that when my mother leaves this earth, be at the funeral acting a damn fool. If God willing, I will be there to remind their ass that they better straighten the hell up. You didn't go see her when she was here so sit your ass down and shut up because the show you are putting on will stop now. Back in the day my family really enjoyed one another. I have never seen any of them ever get into it with one another. My oldest brother we called Jun was the runt of the family. He stood about 5"6 but was the one you would not mess with. He was the big brother, and you knew it. I really don't remember what my brother did for a living, but he always had a job. He loved his Ford mustang and loved my mother; he was a momma's boy for sure. He was married at one point and had three children: a boy and two girls. While my brother was being treated for cancer, I was trying to find help because I didn't want to have happen to my brother what happened to my sister. I was in the Navy at the time and had shipmates that I found out worked at one of the big cancer hospitals in Houston. I asked how I could get my brother there for treatment. They gave me the avenues and I pursued them with all the strength in my body. I finally got him an appointment with an Oncologist there and the red tape that we had to endure to actually get him into the appointment was not what we expected and proved to be a failure of great proportions. Jun died of cancer in 2004, never getting the help that could have possibly saved his life. The worst part was I was not there, and I hate to this day that I wasn't. My sister Tessa was the next to the oldest sibling and was the best big sister ever. I was afraid of her because she was just so tough but was so pretty to me. My sister had three children: 2 boys and a girl. I had taken custody of my niece later on; her sons were grown men. My sister for years worked in food service. One day we as a family went to her house and she told us she had cancer. This was October of 2003, she passed away in December of that year. That is when I took custody of my niece. I was called to come to the hospital because she was not doing well. When I got to the hospital she was in ICU. I walked in the room, and she was dying right before my eyes. The doctors removed me from the room and called code blue. I will never forget what I saw that day, she passed away a few minutes later! While we sat in the hospital mourning my sister's passing, I wanted to shout out "This wasn't supposed to end like this. She was supposed to beat cancer, she was supposed to win!" I buried my sister because I refused to allow my mother to bury a child of hers. After my sister's funeral I was lying in my bed and a commercial came on for a cancer center that was great with the treatment of cancer patients. I remember becoming really angry because I felt like when my sister was going through cancer treatments that the hospital, she was in didn't care about her and that was a part of my sister's decline and death. I was angry because I had never seen this commercial before and if I would have known about this place, I would have asked them for help. One day after her death I was lying in bed asleep I think, and my sister Tessa appeared at my bedroom door. She was wearing a scarf on her head and a hospital gown. I asked her "Are you ok?" She said "Yes." I asked, "Are you sure?" She repeated "Yes." I then said to her "Come and get in the bed." She started walking towards me and when she got close to the bed, she put her hand on the bed. I then grabbed my sister's hand, my sister then disappeared. That was the moment that I finally grieved my sister's death. I cried for hours, and I really mourned her. I hated cancer and I hated what it did to my sister, she did not deserve to die like she did. The worst part is She didn't win, she was not victorious, she lost. I had to bury my sister, the best sister ever was now gone, and I really didn't understand cancer very well. I just knew that it had taken two people that were important to me and no one had real good answers to give. No one could make it make sense to me, I wanted it to make sense! Jay was the brother that I got along with the least, he was mean, and I didn't like that about him. He was the brother that was the real gangster. He was the drug dealer that had several prostitutes that worked for him.

I can remember one time being at his house and going through a draw. I came across some pictures of some young ladies posed in very provocative manners. I asked him who they were, and he said they were his girls. I have so many interesting stories about him. One time when I was in high school, I was on the public bus on my way home. I see this car being chased by the police. I look at the person who had jumped out of the car and was running down the street trying to get away. It was my brother Jay. Yes, he did get away that day. When I got home to my mother, about 30 minutes later he comes walking up full of sweat and breathing hard laughing about what had happened. I think I was about 17 years old when my brother walked into my room as I sat up in my bed and before my brother could tell me I told him I knew that Jay was deceased, I had just saw it in a dream. My brother was gunned down in a house that was not his. No one really knows what he was doing there. There were lots of rumors about his murder, but I was a teenager, and I really didn't know how to follow-up on who killed my brother. So, I spent a lot of years not knowing that the man who killed my brother was in prison for his murder. It had to be shortly after my brother Jay passed away that I was in bed asleep, and I was awakened by the feeling of someone sitting on my bed. When I opened my eyes to see who it was, I was immediately frightened. My brother Jay was sitting at the foot of my bed. I sat up and said, "Jay, I'm scared please don't come back!" He never came back to visit me, but I realized that was his way of letting me know that he was ok. He continued to visit my other brothers and sisters, because when we would have family gathers, they would all talk about him coming to visit. Moving to Houston was a big deal for my family, it was a fresh start, and my brother Gene was in need of that. When he was in Louisiana he was at a party and a fight broke out, he was shot in the leg as an innocent bystander. When Gene got to Houston, he got a job working at McDonalds and moved up in the business. I can remember him being a District Manager and became best friends with Henry who became the owner of at least three McDonalds. After leaving McDonalds he decided to go to another company that did not deal with food and has been there almost 20yrs. Gene was never the brother to get into much trouble he was always on the straight and narrow. He married a few times, had a few kids five to be exact, but he also had kids that he said were his. He was the dad to three others and even adopted one of his ex-wife's sister's daughters. He is just a real solid guy when it comes to family. His current wife I like a lot, they really take care of each other. Tosha came in with three kids two of them that were on their way out and a three-year-old. My brother treats them like they are his kids as well. Tosha makes me laugh all the time and I really enjoy being around her. I am really happy that my brother and her found one another. Gene and Carl were brothers and best friends. I have a favorite picture of the two of them, they were holding hands and they were in their late 40's. When Gene got married it was on Carl's Birthday May 3rd and even though Carl was a little upset at first it makes it so much more special now. After my family moved to Houston, TX my brother Carl got in with a bad crowd and started selling drugs. Carl was really young but was managing to hold his own in the dope world. One day my brother was out and got into an argument with a man on the corner where he sold drugs. My brother was 19 and this man was much older. I don't know what the argument was about, but he shot my brother in the face with a sawed-off shotgun at point blank range. I was very young, but I remember going to the hospital to visit my brother and his mouth was wired shut. When he finally got to come home from the hospital, my mother would grind his food up so that he could suck it through a straw. Have you ever had red beans and rice through a straw? It's really incredible to see. There is nothing like a mother's love for her kids. After my brother went to prison for several years for drugs he came home and really turned his life around. My brother got a great job where he was the manager of a plastic manufacturing company. He had a 401k and was really thriving. He lived with my mother because he had an issue with his heart. Plus, my mom loved having him around. Carl and I had a special relationship; he called me sister and I called him brother. It was our nick names for one another, but Carl and Gene were the closest. Carl collapsed one day, and my brother had to get him rushed to the hospital. That's when we found out that the valve to his heart had a blockage and he had to have it replaced with either a pig valve or an artificial one. The surgery was scheduled, and my brother was ready. He went into surgery, and something happened my brother's blood pressure would not go down, so they had to keep him sedated. My brother's heart stopped beating and he passed away. The one thing that made me the saddest was I found out after he died that he was afraid to have the surgery. That broke my heart to know that my brother died alone and afraid. He was afraid of what was inevitable, leaving us! My brother Gene took it the hardest, I think. They were the last of the oldest brothers and they spent a lot of time together. As I stated before my older brothers and sisters grew up in Louisiana and came to Houston when they were either late teens or early 20's. The youngest of my older siblings was Rod. He was only 8yrs older than me and was a teen when he moved to TX. Rod was just like my brother Jay he sold drugs and had prostitutes. He drove a lot of fancy cars and always had plenty of women. My brother has two daughters that are the same age just a few months apart and two sons that he had with his wife. Rod was close to my sister Tessa. My brother looked out for me when I was in high school and needed cheerleading uniforms, cheer camp, graduation stuff and anything else a high schooler would need. So, when I got orders home, I was happy to help him when he needed it. He needed a rental car and even though I was apprehensive about it I got it for him. He was going to need it for a while, but I don't really remember why. One day I get a phone call from the police saying that my rental had been in a high-speed chase and that it was totaled. My heart skipped a beat and I just wanted to know if my brother was ok. He was in jail and that was all the information they could give me. I find out where they took him and go and pick him up. My brother was banged up pretty good and had a broken wrist. I looked him in the eyes, and I knew something was wrong. I told him I was taking him to the hospital, and I didn't care what he said. On the way to the hospital, he told me what happened with the police. He did go on a high-speed chase with them, and the car spun out of control and was totaled but here is where it gets interesting. When they got to the car, they pulled him out even though they could see he was visibly injured. They started to beat him repeatedly until he passed out. When he came to, he was in jail with a cast on his arm. When I got him to the hospital, I told them that he had been beaten and I think something's wrong with him I just didn't know what. They took Rob in and ran tests on him. His kidneys were failing and if I had not brought him in when I did, he would have died. My brother had to undergo dialysis for several weeks until his kidneys recovered. Once he recovered it was business as usual. He had this old stank ass girlfriend I really can't remember her name; I do but I would never put her name in my book. She looked like a man to me. I really don't know what he saw in her, but she was his ride or die. I just wanted to punch her in the face every time I saw her. My sister was sick with cancer and Rod was struggling with that and he didn't know how to express his sadness. I would go and see him, and we would talk about it, and he was really hurting and was afraid we were going to lose her. We would go to the hospital and sit with our sister for hours and just talk and laugh. Trying to keep her spirits up as well as my family. When we lost our sister, I could see the life in my brother's eyes leave that day at the burial site. I didn't want to believe it, but it was there. He said to me "I want to be with my sister!" I didn't have a response for that. I wanted my sister back as well, but I knew that was impossible. We buried my sister in December and my brother, Rod was dead by March of the next year. His girlfriend said that my brother was on the corner as usual selling his drugs. My brother kept his drugs in a plastic pouch in his mouth and when the cops pulled up on him, he swallowed it and the cops knew he did. So, they held him for a long time knowing that the plastic would dissolve, and the drugs would go into his system. This was not a small amount of drugs. By the time they let him go he was overdosing and was trying to save himself. At the same time the drugs were taking over him. He had barricaded himself in the apartment with the girlfriend who said that she had tried to make him drink milk, but he wouldn't because the drugs had him crazy. He finally passed out on the bed from a massive heart attack. My brother was dead at the age of 38. He was now with his sister, and I could not believe what had happened. He was so sad after my sister passed and I just didn't want to believe that he was going to be next, but I somehow knew that he would be. I buried my brother because again I was not going to let my mother bury any of her children. He was the sixth sibling to leave this earth and I didn't want to hurt anymore. The pain that I felt for my family was deep and you couldn't sooth it with any kind of love, prayers, hugs, or word of encouragement. It was too deep, and I felt tired! I drank an entire bottle of wine and cried until I couldn't cry anymore. It was not just tears for Rod it was tears for my family, the destruction and pain. In the mist of it all is the youngest sibling Londa who is three years younger than me and the baby of the family. We all know how the baby of the family is. They are spoiled and everything must be about them, and she is no different. My mother almost lost her life-giving birth to my little sister. My mother had a stroke while giving birth to her. The doctors asked my mom if anything happened should they save her or the baby. My mom told them to save my sister. So, while my mother recovered in the hospital my sister was taken home by my grandmother. The only reason she took her was because she was light skinned with beautiful curly hair. My mother was in the hospital for several months because of the stroke and her trying to rehabilitate. Once my mother came home, she wanted her child from my grandmother, and she didn't want to give her back to my mother. My mother finally got my sister back and we moved to our own house. My sister and I never got along even as children. She was always getting in trouble, and I think one of the problems was my mother would tell her, "Why don't you act more like your sister!" I think that made her act even more rebellious. My sister had a little boy at the age of 19 and after that became a lesbian. My sister went to prison young and spent I think 3yrs there. I really don't know because I was off in the Navy, and we really didn't talk very much. I felt she stole from me, so, I just didn't want her in my life at that time. Please don't get me wrong I love my sister, I just don't like her very much. I have quite a few girlfriends who have sisters and I truly envy the relationship they have with their sisters. Sometimes things are said and done that you just don't recover from so easily. When I lost my sister Ann, I realize that life is short, and my sister and I should be better to one another. I meant what I said about loving her. She told me the same, she loves me but did not like me. That's fair but we will definitely make the effort of having a relationship with one another. My sister Ann and Jo have been in my life since forever. My sister Ann was my funniest sister. She stood almost 6ft tall and was skinny as a rail. But if she got in your ass, you had a real problem. Ann got married and had two children, a boy, and a girl. One of the funniest things about my sister was this infectious laugh. She made you laugh just listening to her. While I was writing this book my sister found out that she had stage four breast cancer. This is a woman who got a mammogram every year. When they told her they were going to have to take her breast in true Ann fashion she said, "Shit take them ain't nobody sucking on them anyway!" I laughed so hard because that was just who she was. My sister passed away Jan 2, 2022. I didn't get the chance to say goodbye and that hurt so much that I couldn't breathe. If you are a woman especially a black woman reading this, please be relentless about your overall health. Check your breast regularly and go to the doctor and ask questions, it could save your life. Jo worked as a Manager for McDonald's ever since I could remember, I even worked with him when I was a teenager and then he went to work for Frenchy's Chicken as a manager. He married and had children with a woman that took advantage of his kindness. I was really happy when he left her and went on with his life. Sometimes family members have bad habits that you know could bring them great harm and no matter how many times you try to tell them, they just live their lives. That is Jo, he just lived his life. Unfortunately, my brother Jo died April 14, 2022. When I tell you I am so tired of losing my family members! I love my brother and again I was not there because of my job. He died after having hernia surgery, there was some complications and he passed away. Sometimes there is just no happy ending! People leave you unexpectedly, no matter how much you love them! Last but not least I would be remised if I didn't tell you about my brother called, Mother. Now, he is not really my brother, but he was Ann and Jo's brother, and my mother did as much as she could to raise him as well. Mother is his nickname that he goes by. He is loving and funny and will give you the shirt off his back if you need it. Him and my sister Ann were very close. To hear the heartbreak in his voice broke my heart even more. He will do anything in the world for our family, especially our momma. He makes the best barbeque ribs you would ever taste and when I come home to visit, he makes sure that my husband and I get a rack. Even though we are not siblings by blood, he is still my brother. You have met my family and I am not here to relate to you or your family this one is mine. We have not been perfect, but we are family and whatever that entails I will never be ashamed of or make excuses for. Sometimes you have to realize that the struggle is your purpose and I think that it all has made me who I am today. Do I like some of the things I went through, No. Do I wish that it didn't happen, of course? If I could write my life's story before I came here it would have definitely been a different story. If God gave us that option, I think everyone would write a different story. In the end your story is all you have and when you have the opportunity to change it" make it happen!

LETTER TO THE 8 YEAR OLD ME

"The world suffers a lot. Not because of the violence of bad people, but because of the silence of good people." — Unknown

A LETTER TO MY PREDATOR

From the day a girl can understand she is told not to let anyone touch you in your private area. Don't be in a situation that could get you raped or molested. Unfortunately for me I was never told those things and if I was, I have no memory of it. You are every young girl's nightmare. Predator either you don't know, or you just don't give a damn. You take something so precious from a young girl or boy, something that God gives them, and they can never get it back after an encounter with you. You take their innocence, the one thing that every kid deserves to have. I want you to know that when you assault a kid you change their lives forever. The Crimes Against Children Research Center reports that every 1 in 5 girls and 1 in 20 boys are a victim of child sexual abuse. I unfortunately was one of your victims and I am going to tell you what that has done to me and no matter what I will always suffer with this. First of all, I can never look at a little girl with her father, brother, uncle, cousin, or grandfather like normal people do. Let me explain; one day when I lived in Los Angeles, CA and I was out having lunch and I was on the phone with my friend who inspired me to write this book. I was sitting watching this man interact with what I could only assume was his daughter. He was holding his daughter on his lap, and I was so nervous for her because I felt like he was doing something inappropriate with her. The reason for this assumption was because when I encountered you predator you sat me on your lap and while it looked really innocent you were putting your hand under my dress and touching my private area. So, when I see a little girl with a man, I am suspicious of him. As I spoke with my friend, I was describing what I saw, and she was explaining to me that that was completely normal. No one should ever have to explain to a person that a daughter sitting on her father's lap is normal. You destroy everything in your wake and go on as if nothing ever happened, because many young girls never utter a word of the horror they have endured. You feel safe because you know that for the most part no one really tells and for the ones that do most of the time nothing happens. I can remember the time I was a senior in high school, and I was in class alone with my teacher who was a male of course. He asked me to come to his desk and I did because it was almost graduation and I wanted to make sure I was not missing any assignments to graduate. This man stood up and grabbed my face and kissed me as if I was an adult. As I pulled away, he told me that I was beautiful, and he could not resist. I didn't report him because I had already been conditioned at 8 years old not to say anything and so I didn't. Again, predator you have won because we just don't tell. Now, I am going to tell my final and most horrific story of predatory actions. I was probably around 14yrs old, and I had gone to visit my best friend who lived a short bus ride away. While I was at her home I walked across the street and through some abandoned apartments to go and see another friend. While at that friend's house it had started to get dark, so I left to go back to my best friend's house to tell her I was going to go home. As I walked through the abandoned apartment complex it was dark and I was looking down because I am really afraid of snakes, and I didn't want to encounter one on my route. As I'm walking through, I feel a hand on me then I feel myself being jerked so hard that it took my breath away. I could not even scream. I had been snatched into the abandoned apartment complex. There was a stairway before the apartment, so my reflexes made me grab hold and start to scream. As I'm screaming someone puts their hands over my mouth and the other person pries my hands from the railing. I am being drug into an abandoned apartment. Once I get into the apartment, I can see four boys who are now laughing at the terrified me. I try to run away, and they tackle me to the floor. Now, I know they are serious and want to hurt me. The reason I say now I know they are serious is because I knew them from school, and they seem to not care! They drag me into a back room of this apartment and proceeded to take my clothes off. I start to scream again and one of them put their hand over my mouth. I really start to panic because no one could hear me, and no one knew where I was. They are all holding me down while one is trying to get my pants off. I had my legs wrapped together so tight that he could not get them apart. They then started to work on my shirt. It was pulled off and my bra as well. They start playing with my breast and I start moving around trying to get away. At some point I got punched in the face and I started to cry. While on the floor with no shirt or bra on, there is glass on the floor that is cutting into my back. One of the boys takes out his penis because they still could not get my pants off me and starts rubbing my face with it. They were all enjoying the fear they were inflicting on me. I'm too afraid to scream because that is how I got hit the first time so now I'm just fighting to get away. As one is rubbing his penis on my face the others are playing with my breast or between my legs and I am crying. Somehow, I manage to get upright, I grab my shirt bra and a stick and I'm swinging the stick at them and crying. I back out into the main space of the apartment and as soon as I could I took off running. I had my bra and shirt in my hand. I ran as far as I could without stopping and here is where the story gets hazy! I think I caught a bus home, or I ran all the way home. Really to this day I am not sure. Also, when I got home, I think I told my mother about what had taken place, but I am really not sure. If I would have told her, I'm sure she would have called the cops and I would have given their names and where they went to school. I'm sure the cops would have gone to the school and got them, none of that happened. For years I believed that I finally was brave enough to tell that someone hurt me, and the reality is that I didn't. I don't really know what I said for why I was hurt but I believe that if I had told my family those boys hurt me, they would have done everything in their power to make them pay. It's funny how your mind plays tricks on you. Now, I know you're thinking well if your mind plays tricks on you maybe this never happened. Unfortunately, it happened, and I live it over and over in my head. Me being conditioned to not say anything is the part that makes the rest of the story a little blurry. I wanted so bad to believe that I had finally reported someone hurting me, but I hadn't, and another set of predators got away with hurting me again. What makes it even worse is I saw those boys at school all the time and I still never said a word. Just made sure I avoided them at all cost.

To all the predators out there that hurt without remorse, you are worse than any hurricane, tsunami, or tornado that destroys towns, cities, and countries. Those places can be rebuilt after those storms come through. You cannot rebuild the hurt and devastation that you cause. We cannot rebuild after you have come through. We can only move forward and pray that we never encounter another one like you. When it becomes too much for that one person to bear, they attempt the most horrible act that they could imagine. I attempted suicide because the pain was too much to bear. I was 14yrs old and I had had enough of the pain and not being able to share it with anyone. One night I sat on my bed with a bottle of pills. I don't know what they were. I found them in the medicine cabinet in the bathroom and felt like they would do the trick. As I sat on my bed, I could think of no reason to remain here on this earth. It had all been chaos and I wanted it all to end right then. I did not say a prayer. I just got some water and put them in my mouth drank the water and swallowed all 12 of them. I passed out for I don't know how long, but when I came to, I had a really bad headache, and no one had even noticed that I had passed out. I really don't know what part was worse. The fact that I tried to take my own life, or that no one even noticed. I didn't feel that God spared me because I had a purpose, I just felt like I didn't do it right. All I know is that I never tried it again. Just writing about this is giving me great anxiety because I know there are going to be people who judge me because I did this. I really don't care what anyone thinks about my trials and tribulations, because they are mine and I choose to speak my truth. The thought of me not being here today makes me so grateful that God spared me and allowed me to live on. I know now that there was so much life I had to live, and I would have missed it all. I'm grateful every day for blessings that he has bestowed on me. I really hate that I met you predators because you have made a life that should have been filled with innocence, peace and hope a life of fear, pain, and disappointment. I know that is what you do but it all stops here and now! I no longer fear you. I love the fight you gave me, and I will use it forever.

LETTER TO THE 8 YEAR OLD ME

"Many people will walk in and out of your life, but only true friends will leave footprints on your heart." — Eleanor Roosevelt

LETTER TO MY FRIENDS

I added this chapter because this is so important to me. It has always been said that you cannot pick your family, but I'm here to say that you can. I have chosen a family of friends that I feel makes me a lucky woman. After joining the Navy in 1992 I met my best friend of 26yrs. I met my friend Kay at a shipmate's house when I was pregnant with my oldest son. Kay was quiet and of course I was not. We immediately hit it off and tore Norfolk up. Now, when I was pregnant with my son and was about to give birth, Kay came to the hospital to help me. Unfortunately, she couldn't help me because she was too busy about to pass out. I said, "What are you going to do when you have your children?" Her response was, "I'm not having children!" Three children later my friend became a pro. Kay is from New Orleans and definitely made sure you knew it. She is so unapologetically her. When she met her boyfriend at the time who is currently her husband for over 20 something years, she was so mean to him. I told her he was nice, and she should give him a chance. Now, the rest is history. A really cool story about us two. Many years ago, I was living in Los Angeles with my first husband, and I wanted Kay to come visit me. I felt she needed a break, and she did too. So, she flew out and I had all these things planned for us. My husband had agreed to watch the kids all weekend and it was going to be me and my best friend doing it up in LA. I found this club, and everyone knows that you have to have a certain look to get in the clubs in LA. We get into this fancy club, and we are having a grand old time. We get invited to VIP and we are like ok this is great. In VIP is Rick Fox and we are like OMG! We hung out with him, and we took pictures, it was amazing. To this day we will talk about that night. Kay's mom was one of my favorite people. She was so sweet and when she would see me, she would say "Hey my baby!" I had such a love for her mother. Kay's mom passed away in 2021 and I know that devastated my friend. I just wanted to make it better for her and I knew I couldn't. She is my family, and I will always be there for her. Kay was the matron of honor in my wedding, and I was honored. My friend Drea, and I have known one another about the same amount of time as I have known Kay. I met Drea working part time in a department store in Norfolk and she worked there as well. I was the kind of friend you call and say we need to go check a chick and I would be ready in five minutes. Drea helped deliver my son, our sons are a month apart. Drea and I don't really see one another that often but I consider her to be one of my closest friends and family. After getting off active duty I joined the Navy Reserves and moved to Houston. When I checked into my Reserve unit, I met another one of my closest friends. Pat was a reservist as well and we immediately became friends. I was pregnant with my youngest son when I met her, so we have been friends for over 24yrs. Pat and I won't see one another for years but, when we do it's like it was just yesterday when we saw one another last. She was the maid of honor in my wedding, and she made sure that from the bridal shower to my bachelorette party everything was perfect. Pat married an amazing person that makes her happy and I am so very happy for her. We are both grandparents and love the moments of being with our grandchildren. I also met a really close friend by the name of Shey, around the same time that I met Pat. Shey has been a great friend for years. Someone I can call on when I need help. My mother was diagnosed with dementia, and she helped me get information for an aid to come and help with my mother. If I needed her to go and check on my mom she does. These are people that I hold close to my heart. I got a job with and investment company when I first moved back to Houston and these two ladies have been in my corner ever since. I don't talk to them often but when I tell you we love one another we do! Kat was the friend that gave me the nickname LaLa. I love that name and really, she is the only person that calls me that to this day. She and I became fast friends after meeting when I started working for AIM, an investment company back in the day. Ang and I had kids the same age, so our kids played together all the time. Ang retired from the Army as a Warrant Officer, and I use to tease her all the time about the difference between the Navy and Army. We both where reservist back then and when she would go out on her two weeks training, she was in the field, and I would be at a really nice hotel ordering room service. If anyone of these ladies called me and said I need you I would be on the next thing smoking. We have watched one another kids grow up to be fine young men and women. As I said I have friends that I consider to be really close, but we don't get to see one another that often. This would also be one of those friends that I love dearly. Tonj is the friend I met when we both were hired at Chase bank many years ago. When I met her, she had a boyfriend and they wanted to get married. I had moved from Houston to Los Angeles and my friend called and asked if I would go with them to Vegas so that they could get married. Of course, they came out and we went to Vegas, as we stood in line, I'm telling people not to do it, that they are making a big mistake. The great part is my friends have been married for over 20yrs now. They have three beautiful children that I love dearly. When we talk, we never miss a beat, because that is what friendship is. I became a recruiter in 2003 and I put this young lady in the Navy. Now, funny story, the night before she was to go to MEPS, we were out partying that entire night. We ended up staying up until it was time for her to go process. She went in the club clothing she had on that night.

I call her Slim and we have been friends ever since. Now, she is my crazy friend though. She is the friend you call when you want to push someone down. I went through a very tough situation, and she was like "you want me to go and turnover his equipment?" Of course, I said no but if I would have said yes, his shit would have been on the floor. She makes me mad too though. She can be so mean, and she hates when I check her on it. So, when I got married her mom came to me and said, "find my daughter a husband". I don't think I took her serious, but I guess it was always in the back of my mind. Well, fast forward a few years ago I went home to visit and of course my friend and I got together as per usual. We took a picture together as we always do, and I posted it on Facebook. One of my Sailors saw her picture and immediately called me and asked who that was. I explained it was an old friend. He wanted to know if it was ok for him to call her. I asked Slim and she of course wanted to know what he looked like. We went to his Facebook page, and she agreed he could call. They started dating and they have been married almost two years now. She was in my wedding, and I was in her wedding. Even though we fight I would not trade our friendship for anything. Now, this next friend as I have said earlier is the reason this book even exists. Riss and I have been friends since 2003 and I can say that she makes me own all my shit. She does not let me get away with anything. If I say or do something crazy, she will check me on it, and I do the same for her. I think everyone needs that friend that will give you that needed chin check when you need it. I have to tell this story because it is so funny. Riss travels a lot because she is retired and no matter where I am stationed, she is going to come and visit. So, when I was stationed in Phoenix she came often to visit. On one of her visits, I had just washed my hair and I was in the mirror putting the finishing touches on it. She was lying in the bed, but her cell phone was on my dresser which was a little way away from my bed but not too far if you sat up in the bed. Some extra info about this situation, Riss is tall, so her limbs are long. Also, my bed sits up really high off the floor. Riss wanted her phone so lying down she attempted to reach for it.

As she reaches, she scoots a little further off the bed. Well, she loses her balance and falls off the bed onto the floor. I said before my bed sits really high. I hear a thud then some grumbling. She likes to say I said to her without even stopping curling my hair "Did you fall out the bed?" While I'm doing this, she says I'm laughing. I don't remember laughing but I did ask her if she fell and continued to curl my hair. I love my friend though; I wouldn't change a thing about us. I went from reserve to active duty recruiting in 2005 and that is when I met my friend Lo she had just got in recruiting, and she just had this great spirit about her. We became fast friends, and she was now a part of my circle of family friends. We have seen one another through some difficult times and we both have come out on the other side victorious. I am so very proud of her. She has an amazing career and manages to have fun while doing it. When I was feeling sorry for myself, she put things in perspective for me. We both love to eat so that is our thing. We will find a great place to enjoy food and beverage. I wanted Lo in my wedding so bad, but she was on deployment and missed it. We are also travel buddies, though we have not traveled in a while when we did, we had amazing times. We don't get to see one another often but when we do there is always a great time. Some people say that having a lot of friends is not good. I say it's amazing. I get to have this network of people that care about me and me about them. When I was stationed in LA in 2010,

I met two people that made living there bearable. Kate and Tosh are two of the kindest women I have ever met. I met them in Bebe the store's dressing room. I was trying on a dress, and they complimented me on it. We all exchanged numbers and started hanging out soon thereafter. They taught me a lot about LA life. I was single and navigating being single out there was not for the faint of heart. These women didn't know me from anyone off the street, but they took me in as a friend and when I was sick took care of me. I got to see some amazing places in LA because of these two beauties. We also, don't get to see one another often but when I got married these ladies flew from LA to Houston to witness my union, that's love. I also met a young lady in LA that is a forever friend that just may be my kin. We share the same last name, and her family is from my hometown. So, we met because I needed a new phone and my boyfriend at the time went with me to the cellphone store and she was a manager there. Eve could see through his bullshit and when we became friends, she told me. Our kids went to the same school and became friends. Her daughter has grown up to be an outstanding young woman. Eve flew to my wedding and when I needed help creating my bridesmaids' bouquets her and my best friend stayed up half the night to help. I have this friend, that I met working in Inglewood, CA and we are still close friends to this day. Jay and I worked together and did a lot of traveling together. When I say travel, we probably were in Vegas almost every weekend. We would have such an amazing time. One of the last weekends we spent in Vegas was when I found out I had been selected to Chief, we went to Vegas to celebrate. She took me through my Chief season, and I wanted to kill her on a many of days. Our relationship survived the season and when I got married, she flew to Texas to be a part of my amazing day. We didn't talk for a while and I wasn't sure if we were still friends, but because we sat down with one another and talked we repaired the broken parts of our friendship. That is what friendship is about. When it is broken you fix it. I love our relationship; it has smooth and rough places, and we still understand the love we have for one another. I got stationed in Phoenix and I met this woman, and in the beginning, we did not like one another. She thought I was too much, and I didn't like her attitude. Fast forward we both get selected to Chief Petty Officer. What we went through added a bond that could never be broken. She is one of my closest friends. If she called and said I need your help I would be on the next thing smoking. We have shared things that just can't be explained. I remember a situation where our boss really didn't care for me, and he made that known. He really liked Rea and he also made that known. So, one night we were at an event, and he said in front of me to Rea you need to watch who you hang with. I understand how the recruiting game goes so I wanted to let her off the hook. I told her look if hanging with me is negatively going to affect you, let's just not hang at work so that you don't keep getting these crazy conversations. She was like no you are my friend; I don't give a fuck what they think. I have a real respect for that situation because she could have taken that out. While in Phoenix we had a Chief Select come through that I knew could hang with us. She made it through the season and was now a Chief. I knew we would be friends. We had an election and as I stated before leadership didn't care for me, and she was the only one that voted for me when I ran for treasure. Sometimes when you show weak ass people, you're not afraid of them they try to flex. It only works on people who give a damn. That's just a little information for the people that need it. We are both Virgos, so we get one another. Last but surely not least is my friend Sam. A really funny story about our friendship. We had to drive from Orlando to Jacksonville for work and that makes for a long day. My friend has a lot of hair, but she likes wear wigs. While on our way back she was messing with it and kept adjusting it. So, at some point she could not take the wig anymore. I was driving and this girl grab that wig off her head and hear is where it became the funniest moment I have witnessed. She pulled out her phone and went to YouTube found the taps sound and played it for the wig because she was throwing it away. I laughed so hard I couldn't breathe. We have such an organic friendship, I have only known her for a few years but the bond we have unfortunately is one of grief, but it makes our friendship really special.

When you speak of your pain, and you have someone that knows that pain the conversation is different. You never want anyone to feel that kind of pain because it's deep and it destroys. She is strong like me, and I appreciate the fact that she trusted me with her hurt. I told her you're bruised not broken. I write this letter to you friends to let you know how much you mean to me. We have always been there for one another, and it feels my heart with joy. You are my family of friends and I thank God for you. Thank you for being the friend I needed you to be. Just know that even if we never speak again I still and will always call you friend.

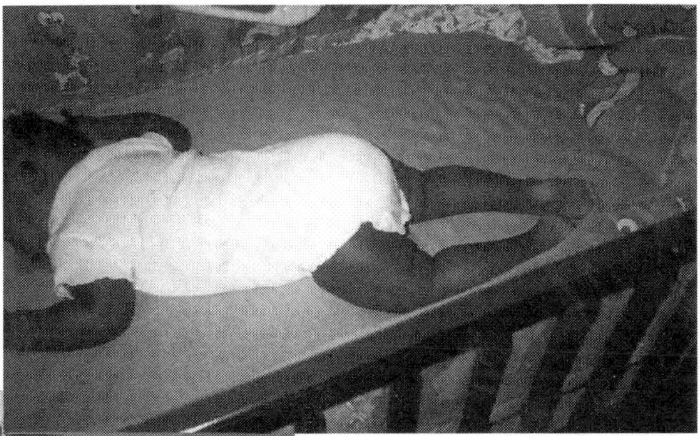
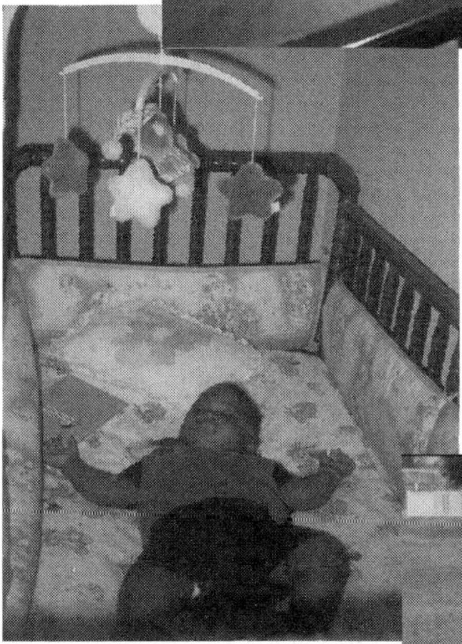
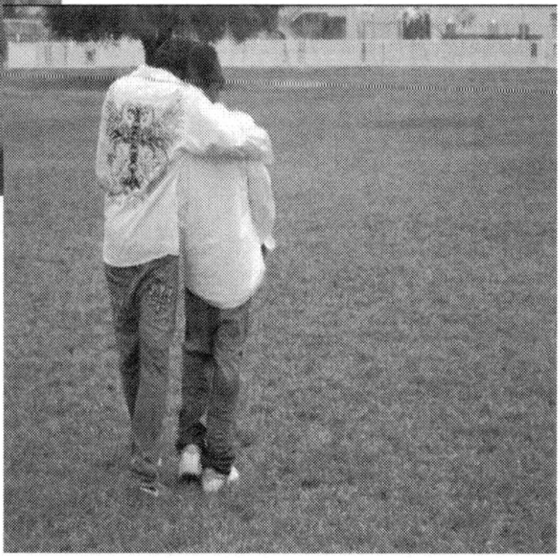

LETTER TO THE 8 YEAR OLD ME

"Always remember, you are braver than you believe. Stronger than you seem, smarter than you thin and loved more than you know" _{mom}

LETTER TO MY SONS

Let me start by saying you two are the best thing that could have come into my life. All I ever wanted to do was protect you. Tee you are my first born and you where trial and error. Let's be clear there was a lot of errors. First, of all I was not prepared to have a kid at the age of 23, and when I brought you home, I was ill equipped to handle you. So, the hospital in their infinite wisdom sent a nurse to come and help me the first couple of weeks.

Let's be real they were just making sure that I didn't kill you. I loved you so much! I would sometime just sit and stare at you and kiss your little feet. I cried a lot after you were born because, I was sad. I felt like I was going to disappoint you. I was not married, and I had this little boy that I was responsible for. I didn't want to fail at this because your life depended on it. You were mine and I had the responsibility of raising you. I was so afraid that I would mess that all up, but I was determined to get it right. No one was going to hurt you like I was hurt. So, I kept my eyes on you like a hawk. I made sure that at an early age you and your brother knew that there was nothing that you could not tell me. In your later years that bit me in the ass, but I think it worked out well. I have a funny not so funny story about you as a two-week-old baby. This is when I knew I had real work to do. I had laid you on the couch so that I could go and get your bottle. At two weeks old you rolled off the couch onto the floor. I heard this loud thump, and I came running. You and I started crying and I swore that day that I would never let you fall again without me being there to pick you up. I wonder if you two remember when we had the sex talk. How I showed you and your brother pictures of what could happen if you didn't use protection. I said to you both, "When you are ready to have sex to come to me so that I could take you to the store and get you some protection". Unfortunately, when you came to me at 16yrs old and stated you were ready I was not ready. We went to the drug store, and I took you to the contraceptive aisle where I let you pick what you needed. I wanted to go running out of the store, but I knew you would be safe because I had given you all the tools you needed to do so. When you called me to tell me about your orgy that you had in Singapore, all I could say was that's nice. I had taught you all your life there was nothing you couldn't tell me, and you really believed it. You have such an amazing presence and I know that life gets hard sometimes but I promise you that you will figure it all out. I trust in the man that you have become. You joined the Navy, and I am so proud because you had followed in mine and your father's footsteps. The Navy assisted me in turning you into a man and I will forever be grateful. Understand that the Navy was a chapter in your life and God has something bigger and better for you. I wish that you had a better relationship with your father. I know that sometimes it gets hard, and you need to hear a man's perspective. I hope that you know that even though Ray did not raise you, he loves you like a son and you can go to him. I will always be here to catch you when you fall, I promise. You have had an opportunity to go places young men and women your age will probably never get to. Use what you have gotten from the Navy to create your future. Life is a series of events, some good, some bad. What you must do is take those moments and build, learn, and grow. I told you a long time ago that I could not tell you how to be a man, but what I could do is tell you what it takes to be one. You must always be responsible and take care. If you do those things, you will be fine. This is a new chapter don't be afraid of it, embrace it you have everything that it takes to be successful. Remember when you said, "Mom I want a guitar." You took two lessons and then you just mastered it. That is what life is, mastering the things that you are good at. Now, when you play it, it's effortless to you and to me you sound like the people that make millions of dollars playing. Keep your beautiful head up to the stars and you will eventually get there. Milton, my baby boy and the one person that single handedly know how to push my buttons. The bond we have is so strong, but you are always trying to act so tough. My favorite nickname for you is the one your uncle Los gave you, Lil Bill. It's so funny how you really looked like that little cartoon character when you were a kid. I had this mother thing down when you came along so it was effortless trying to raise you. You made it so difficult sometimes. I really don't understand why. I know that you had some issues with people talking about your skin color and that made me so sad. There was nothing that I could do to fix other people that made you feel bad, but I could definitely make sure that you understood your worth. I can remember when we moved to New Orleans, and you started attending the High School there. Living in Los Angeles you never had an issue with anyone saying anything about your skin color. We lived in a predominately white area and to me either you were black or white. I don't think the light or dark of your color mattered, but I could be wrong. All I know is you never came to me with the issue. You finally told me that you were being bullied about your skin color. That broke my heart because you told me they called you a burnt chocolate chip cookie and you were upset. I put you and your brother in the car and we went for a ride. Every time I wanted to talk to you and your brother about something serious, I put you guys in the car, and we went for a ride. I told you that day that your skin color was amazing and that you were handsome, and you would have to start beating girls off with a stick. I wanted you to know that your color was beautiful and that being dark skin was a blessing. I did not want you to have the same negative feeling I had about my skin color when I was growing up. One of the funniest stories I have about you was when you were about 14yrs old you wanted to be just like your brother. So, at the time Tee had dreads and every few weeks we would have family day were I would retwist his dreads and we all would watch a movie. Well on this particular day you were taking a shower and I was retwisting your brothers' dreads. You come out of the shower naked with the towel around your neck calling yourself naked lad. Then you proceeded to tell me how you wanted your penis to be just as big as your brothers. I really had no words and to add to it, I look down at your brother and he smiles and nods his head like "yep!" I wanted to laugh so bad, but I felt like that would have been so inappropriate. Mickey you are going to be ok son I know it. I know that I am constantly in your ass but that's because I don't want to worry about you. That is one of the main reasons I wanted you to join the Navy. I know that you must find your own path but as your mom I just want to make sure that the path you choose is the one that will sustain you. When I found out you were having a kid the day, he was being born I was hurt. The part that hurt the most is you didn't trust my love for you. Yes, I was going to be upset but my love for you would have gotten us through it. My grandson is the best thing in the world. I love that little boy like I love you. There is nothing I won't do for him in hopes that I can help him navigate and be successful in this world. He is the best part of you and his mother. I want him to identify with both of his cultures. Being have black and Mexican is a gift that I want him to cherish. I hope that he will find his way in this world, and I hope that he allows me to help along the way. Whatever you feel you didn't get from your father I want you to make sure that Kai gets. Every time I look at that little boy, I see you and all the dreams I had for you. I want you to always encourage him to follow his dreams and be the best version of himself. It is about breaking the cycle. I broke the cycle in my family, and I want to make sure you do the same. I am so proud of you following your dreams. I hope that you get what your heart desires son. I admire the fact that you kept pursuing your dream to play professional football. If you get the opportunity to play, I'm your biggest fan. Life is a challenge and you have shown me on several occasions that you are up for it. Don't ever let anyone tell you what you can't do, because you have all the tools you need to be whatever it is you choose to be. You and your brother have been everything that I could ever asked for. I know I'm hard on you both, but it is because you are a black man growing up in a white world. I can remember a conversation I had with a white woman about the difference in conversations that we have with our children when they leave the house. I was saying that she has never had to tell her children if the police pull you over make sure before they get to the car to have your insurance card and ID on the dash and your hands on the steering wheel. If at any time during the stop they ask you to get anything out of the glove compartment you take the ticket and just fight it in court. If you are not sure why we do this, it's because when black men make moves to open or look for anything they are more than likely shot and killed because the officer feels he is going for something to hurt them. I don't know what I would do if someone harmed either one of you. I write this chapter to you to let you know that everything I do or did is for your benefit. I know that sometimes it didn't feel like it, but rest assure that it was. Every day I pray for you both, that God watches over you and that he continues to protect and bless you in your walk on this earth.

Continue to come to me and I will always be there to help you navigate this life. I will leave you with this quote that I heard some years ago and I have added it to my toolbox of life. Bloom where you are planted Sons!

LETTER TO THE 8 YEAR OLD ME

"I've made mistakes in my life. I've let people take advantage of me, and I accepted way less than I deserve, but I've learned from my bad choices and even though there are some things I can never get back and people who will never be sorry, I'll know better next time and won't settle for anything less than I deserve." unknown

LETTER TO THE 48 YEAR OLD ME

Hey girl, you ready for this? I'm about to get really real with you and I know you're not going to like it. I'm tired of this and I know that you are too. Let's get through it together. Just know that this is love in its rarest form. A lot of people are going to judge you harshly after this chapter and I know how fragile you are. It's ok, I judged you as well and we both know how that turned out. Promise me that you are going to continue to stand tall and own your shit. It's yours and they have no idea how hard this is going to be. This is our season to heal and heal we will. Ok, if you don't want to look at me differently, please skip this chapter and go on to next because shit's about to get real! Ok, let's start with who we are now, then we can go back to where it began. Looking in the mirror naked, I focus on the flaws because that is all I see in me. All the scars internal and external. The internal ones are the most prominent and noticeable. I can pick myself apart in 2.2 seconds. The sad part is, I do it. I know the parts of me that I hate. Yes, hate is a strong word and I assure you I have used it in the proper context. I had an underlined hate for myself. I can come across confident and secure but deep inside I'm a scared little girl and I just want to be safe. I stood in the mirror naked one day and said find all the things that are great about you, and you are not putting on any clothing until you do! I stood there for about 20 minutes with nothing to say. Can you believe that I looked at my beautiful self and had nothing beautiful to say? But if I wanted to say something negative, I got it all day. So, I decided I was not moving, and I meant I was going to get my shit together because I deserved it. I started with you have incredibly beautiful legs. Your body is sexy, and you have an amazing smile. I went on to talk about how my dark skin looked like creamy caramel and my hair was the hair of the Gods. I really started to get into it, it felt good. I asked myself a question "Who am I?" As I thought about the question, I pondered on the answer because honestly, I didn't know who I was. I knew who I wasn't and that was not ok. Here is who I am and working to be. I am confident. I know who I am and what I want from people, and I know what I will allow from them. I'm confident enough to know that if they want me in their world, they will take all of me. I am flawed; I know that I am not perfect, but I am perfectly imperfect. I saw all my flaws and I wore them like a badge of honor. I would see my flaws in other people then pick them apart. It was not on purpose it was so subconscious that my friend told me that was what I would do. I had to realize what I was projecting was what I rejected about myself. I don't always do the right thing or say the right thing but know I am always working on that part of me. I don't always do the right thing. I'm going to leave that right there. I am kind; it takes very little effort to put a smile on someone's face. You never know what a person is going through inside. A kind word or gesture could turn yours or their day around. Kindness is not being a fool for people, it's being understanding of people and caring about them despite them. I am beautiful; this may sound vain to you, but

I don't really care. I am beautiful and I know that now. I don't have to be ashamed of feeling that way about myself. I can remember when someone would say that to me, and I would be surprised that they thought I was beautiful. I was home visiting family and one of my molesters had died and because I was home, I had to attend his funeral. My aunt by marriage who had not seen me in years said to me, "You turned out to be a beautiful young woman because you were such an ugly little girl!" The same gasp you just did I did as well, but I did it inside. What she didn't know was I was struggling with that beautiful woman she saw because the little girl inside of me was ugly. So, now I own my beauty. It's mine. I am powerful; and I know that my power is what makes me who

I am today. The power in me is what makes me get up every day and try a little harder to become the person I want to be. When you are going through a storm you need your inner power to get you through. Power is the faith within that may be the size of a mustard seed but is enough to move a mountain. I think I have always looked for the security of a relationship to complete me. It took a long time to realize that I was enough all by myself. When I was a young woman, I dated this guy who was about 12yrs my senior. He showed me the attention I wanted, and I was not in love, but I was really in like. He did all the romantic things and I thought he was great. Then I got pregnant, and the real person came out. When no one knows your truth, it is really easy to fall victim.

I gained a lot of weight with my oldest son, and he would make comments about how big I was, and it would hurt my feelings. I wouldn't say anything and just suffer in silence. One day he called me a beach whale and I was devastated. He thought all these things he was saying were funny! I was miserable in my own home and was sure that it was going to get worse. One night he left for work, and I was up watching TV and a commercial for KFC came on. I was about five months pregnant at the time and my cravings were insane. I wanted KFC, I got in my car and drove to where it was. It was right across the street from my fiancé's job at the time. For whatever reason, I got my food and before I went back home, I drove through the parking lot of his job to see if his car was there.

Guess what, it was not, and he left home like he was going to work. When he gets home, I ask him how was work and of course he said it was fine. So, for a few nights when he said that he was going to work I would wait awhile then go by and see if his car was there. I was completely over it. I confronted him and told him he would no longer sleep in my bed because he could give me and my child a disease with what he was doing. One night in my sleep I dreamt that he was asleep on the couch, and I got out of bed went into the kitchen retrieved a knife, walked into the living room and got on top of him and started stabbing him repeatedly. I woke up the next day and told him that I was leaving and that he could stay. I got my own apartment at five months pregnant and had my son four months later. Ok, one down and a few more to go and you will see the pattern that took me years to see. I had my son in September of 1995 and a few months later I met my ex-husband. I was afraid and I had a newborn. He said that he would take care of me and my son. I was like great because I can't do this on my own. We got married a year later. The first time it happened we were getting a new house and he had left his work shoes at the old house, so he needed to go get them. I said that I would ride along with him. When he got in the car his phone rang and he answered of course. In the car you can hear conversations on phones because there is no outside noise, and this was before there was Bluetooth. I could hear a woman's voice and he was trying to have a general conversation with her, and I guess she could tell by his answers that I was in the car. I could hear her say "Is your wife with you?" of course he replies with yes. I didn't say a word, but I was fuming inside! We get home and I'm plotting on how I'm going to catch his ass. He goes to sleep, and I get his beeper and look at all the numbers that came across his beeper. Then I get his cell phone and check for the same number then I write it down. The next day he gets up I iron his uniform and he goes to work. I get my phone and call the number. She answers and I ask her what the nature of business with my husband is. She tells me that his co-worker introduced her to him because he is dating her cousin. I know who this co-worker is, it's his best friend. I get dressed and I head to his office. Ok, this story is how I got the nickname Hurricane. I get there and this friend and my husband are in the office with a few more of the employees. I go in and I go the hell off! I told him that I didn't need him fixing my husband up with a bitch. If he is going to fuck up, you let him find his own bitch to fuck up with! He doesn't need you to fucking help! We moved on from that because you want your marriage to work. If I'm going to be real and tell my story I have a few more to tell about my marriage. Sometime had elapsed, and I was working at a local black owned bank as an accounting assistant. It was a great opportunity for me to get in the banking business and learn the ends and outs of banking. My boss was an older good-looking black male who was married as well. Because we worked together, we did a lot of talking about our marriages. Of course, his marriage was in trouble and mine was too. We bonded over bullshit and drinks. I wrote him a letter about how I was feeling about him. I didn't give it to him. I had it in my briefcase at home. I went to bed and my husband went through my briefcase and found the letter. I woke up to a knife to my throat. We fought the entire night and I had to go to work the next day. My husband actually came up to my office with our baby to meet the guy I wrote a letter to. I was so scared that he was going to make a scene at the bank I could not breathe, and I would have deserved it. When you do tit for tat no one wins. I promise! This story ended my marriage 17yrs ago. My husband had received orders to Los Angeles for recruiting and at this time our marriage was shaky, and I had an amazing job with an investment company. I was not going to go; I went to my mother, and she told me that this is your husband, and you will follow your husband. So, I left my job, my family and friends and moved to LA. My husband left before us to get a place and get settled in so that we could come later. He told me that he had found a babysitter and a friend for me. The boys and myself get to California and I meet the babysitter and my new friend. She seemed to be a nice woman and the babysitter was her mother which was nice. The mother was watching her daughter's kids as well as mine. It gave my boys someone to play with. I was in a new place, and I was happy to have a friend to hang out with and talk to. I started to see things, but I ignored them because I didn't want to believe what my woman's intuition was telling me. My friend was dating this really handsome guy, but she didn't really seem that interested. So, one day I asked her what her perfect man looks like. She described my husband to a tea. When I told my husband about it, he just brushed it off as it could have been anyone. I let it go and moved on. Well, one night she invited me out to go to LA to a club and hang out. I of course said, "Ok." We get to the club, and we are having an amazing time. She meets this guy, and they talk for the remainder of the evening leaving me alone to hang around the club. At the end of the evening, she asks me if I would follow him to his place for her that it was just up the street from the club. She rode with me because I was not familiar with the area, and she was the GPS. I agreed to follow, and we left the club. First of all, it was not down the street it was in Compton, LA. At that time, I drove an all-black SUV with dark tinted windows and this girl had me driving through Compton at 2 a.m. It was more like 20min away and I was pissed. She says give me a few minutes. I'm going to go upstairs with this guy I will return in about 10min. I'm sitting in my car scared and her friend sends out his friend to keep me company. I'm sitting in my car talking with a complete stranger. At some point we both fall asleep. She comes out eventually and we go home. I was so pissed that after that night I no longer had anything to say to her. On the ride back home, I tell her how I didn't appreciate her putting me in that situation knowing that I was married and had a husband to go home to. I, to this day don't know why I didn't just leave her ass and go home. Sometime had gone by and I was riding with my husband somewhere I really don't remember. My husband asked me why I was not talking to my friend anymore. I felt it was time to tell him the truth about what happened that night and that she was not a person I wanted to have in my life. This man, my husband said to me, "Oh I knew about that, but she said all of that was you!" So, you allowed a woman to tell you that your wife went into a house with a man, and you thought it would be a great idea not to say anything to the woman you share a bed and a life with! First of all, you are my spouse and you allowed someone to tell you something about me and you don't think you should talk to me about it. That to me means that you believed what she told you. Second, there is no way someone could tell me something like that about him and I not have gone to him and had questions. Thirdly, I was very disturbed by this level of don't give a damn. I knew that our marriage was in a bad place after that. I called her on the phone and told her if I saw her that I was going to kick her ass on sight. Needless to say, she made sure that I never saw her ass again. After the events of September 11, 2001, my reserve unit was mobilized, and I was sent to San Diego. My husband was left to take care of the kids while I figured out what was going to happen with my unit. I told my husband do not have that girl in my home while I'm away. One day I called home to talk to my husband and the boys, my youngest son answered the phone. I asked where was daddy and his brother? I really don't remember the answer, but I asked if the young lady I specifically said not to have in my house had been in my house. That is not how I asked the question to my son, but you know where I'm going with this. My baby said yes, she had been there a lot. I was angry and I was over this situation. I was about to be sent to Iraq, but I was thinking about my relationship that was not where I wanted it to be. My Lieutenant was someone I could talk to, so I confided in him about what was happening in my relationship. One day he came to me and said, "If you want to leave California and go home to Texas you need to leave now because there will be a stop loss shortly. Meaning I would not be able to leave my reserve unit and transfer to Texas to another unit, I would have to go to Iraq. I decided that it was over, and I was going home. I went home and told him it was over, and I was done with all the betrayal. I buy plane tickets and fly my kids to my mothers in Houston, TX. I fly back to pack the things that I was taking with me. I get back and he has moved this hoe in. I pour bleach on his and her clothes and shoes and took his play station to give to my children. I got a trailer attached to my SUV, loaded up the things I wanted and got on the road from Southern California to Texas. Looking back at this situation, I want you to know I am not bashing my ex-husband. I am speaking my truth. The truth is I was broken, and I found a broken man. At the time I didn't know that I was broken or even what that was. When you look in the mirror you see your reflection. That to me is how attractions work. I attract what I feel I am. Unfortunately, it took me a very long time to figure that out. I moved to Houston to get my life together and do something great. I went out one night with a childhood friend to a club called Maxwell and that is where I met him. He was a handsome man with a gift of gab. I found myself really interested in him because he seemed fun. I needed fun at that point in my life. I'm in the middle of getting a divorce and it seemed to be a great idea to get involved with someone, well you're about to find out how that turned out. We start to date and in the beginning it was great. He was romantic and sweet and that made me happy. I was in school at that time working on my degree and had been hired on active duty recruiting. My children were getting adjusted to living in Texas. I had met his mother and stepfather as well as his father and stepmother. They all were wonderful people and they liked me as well. We would go on road trips together and that felt good. We also loved to dance. We both enjoyed two stepping and we danced really well together. As the relationship went on things started to change and I could see that clearly. Just wanted to believe that I was just seeing things because I had just ended a marriage that was not so healthy. One day I went to lunch with my coworkers at one of my favorite restaurants and as we enjoyed our food, I surveyed the place. I see from afar my boyfriend having lunch with a woman I didn't know. At first, I did not say anything because I didn't want my coworkers to know but mainly, I was embarrassed. I mustered up enough courage and said to my all-male crew "That's my man over there having lunch with some strange woman that I don't know." After they removed the look of shock from their faces they said, "go find out what's going on!" I walk over and the look on his face when I walked up told me everything I needed to know. Yet I still asked the question and of course he lied through his fucking teeth. The woman he was with just sat there and stared at me. Without making a scene I walked back over to my table, and we finished lunch. When he came over that night we talked, no let's be real we argued and then made up. Here's the thing when I let that slide it just got worse. That's because I let him know when I forgave the first bullshit, I would continue to forgive. I had to realize for myself it wasn't going anywhere and end the relationship. How I ended it you say, well, I packed all the things he had at my house in a box, put him in my car and drove him to his home, and there is where I left him. Now, I'm divorced living in Houston, and I have opened my own business. I opened a boutique that caters to mostly women, but I had men clothing and shoes as well. I really loved my store. I went into business with my nephew and sometimes you just can't do business with family. We still love one another but business I will not do with family anymore. They had this cool lounge in third ward not too far from my shop and so he and I went in on advertising together. It was doing great, and I was excited about where my business was going. One night I went to his place and there was this tall handsome guy standing up against the wall and I took notice of him. He finally came over and introduced himself and we exchanged numbers after talking the majority of the night. The next time I saw him he came to my shop, and we went to lunch. I liked his conversation, and it didn't hurt that he was good looking. He worked for a bank in the mortgage department, so I was not worried about his finances. He had a son and a son's mother. We date for about a year and I get orders to transfer to Los Angeles. I prepare to close my store to move. It was heartbreaking for me because it was my dream. He decided that he was going to move to Los Angeles with me. Before we left for LA, his son was turning five and his mom was throwing him a birthday party. He took me to the party, and I thought those women were going to kick my ass. I sit at the table with all the women, and I got rapid fire question after question. That is when I find out that he was still with her when he and I started dating and that he lied and told her he was moving to LA for a job and not to be with me. You would have thought I would have broken it off and said you clown get the hell away from me. But no, I was like let's go. We move to LA in July of that year, and I get to work. He finds a job about 2 months later. Everyone knows it's expensive to live there. The rent was ridiculous and now he was paying half. I thought life was good. My children were happy and so was I. One night in October changed everything and I had only lived in LA three months. He had worked that day and then called and told me that he was attending an event for the bank he currently worked for that evening. I was cool I would just see him later. I fall asleep and wake up around 3 a.m. and he is not home. I immediately get worried because I know we had only been living there a short time and I didn't know if something had happened to him. I called his phone no answer, so I called the jails and hospitals. No one by his name had been admitted. So, now I'm curious. I call his phone again and it goes to voicemail again. I start to think what's important to him because that is going to be his passcode. I figure that out and open his voice mail. The first message is from a woman who was upset with him for just fucking her and leaving. No, I can't make this shit up. I get her number and write it down because I'm about to give her a call. Yes, I called her, and she didn't answer at the time, but she called me back at about 6 a.m. In the mist of all this, I forgot to tell you we had gotten engaged. I was wearing a beautiful ring on my finger. So, now I'm on the phone with the lady that he fucked and left, and she is telling me how they met and that she did not know that he had a fiancée. See the pattern here, I hope so because it took me a long time to see this shit. He comes home around seven something in the morning and tells me this grand story about getting too drunk and getting a hotel to sleep it off. What a surprise when I told him I talked to the woman he fucked and left. I'm so sorry I was drunk, and it will never happen again. The funny thing I have so many stories that I could tell you after this one it would make your head spin. Again, I forgave the first offense which opened the door for the rest of them. Then he became abusive which no one thinks that they will be in an abusive relationship. We began to fight one another, and it was always another woman involved. He had grown fond of this woman because he had given her our home number and she called my house. I informed her that if she ever called my house again that I would find where she lived and beat the dog shit out of her. I told him I was going out one night and I left. I was waiting on him to leave and then I followed him. He went to my favorite little restaurant bar and was meeting the bold one. That's what I called her. I waited until they were together, and I walked up to them and said, "You better be glad I like my career because you both would be picking your teeth up off the floor right now and I would be going to jail!" That night he went to jail for a DWI and when he called me, I told him to call the bitch he allowed into our relationship to come and get his ass out. Needless to say, I didn't go get him from jail and she did. A few weeks later I flew home to Houston for the weekend, and he was supposed to watch the boys for me until I returned. I had attached a tracker to his car and when I returned that Sunday, I plugged it into the computer, and he had spent the entire weekend with this woman leaving my kids home alone the entire weekend. That was it, we had a big fight and I'm not proud of what I said but I said what I said! We were arguing back and forth about how he wasn't shit and he said to me, "Fuck you, suck my dick!" So, I replied, "You come over here and suck my dick because I'm the man in this bitch!" Now, for clarification, I do not have a penis it was a metaphor. That was the final straw for me, I needed peace. We had officially become roommates and I was over it. I made plans to move out at the end of the year because I wanted to save a little more money. He flew his son's mother and her other kids to LA to go to Disney. He didn't ask if my kids wanted to go. So, while he was at Disney that weekend, I moved out. I left his ass with that expensive apartment that I knew he couldn't afford by his damn self. He came home that Sunday and called me. He said, "Did you move out?" Yep! Figure out how you're going to pay that shit by your damn self. I was over him and the bullshit he was putting me through. In the process of all that the woman he was seeing kept calling me telling me how I must have not been good enough that's why he was with her. I told her honey; you think you got something! I can't wait until you find out you don't have shit and when you do, you're going to call and apologize to me. Six months later I received a call from her cursing at me telling me to leave her Facebook page alone and then she hung up. I called her back and proceeded to explain to her that I had not thought of or cared about her or him since I moved out. She then tells me the story of him flooding her house by plugging the bathtub and running the water. Then he tried to get a restraining order on her so that he could get her removed from her house where she paid the mortgage. Lastly before she got him out of the house, she said she kept smelling pee in her bedroom and she couldn't figure out where the smell was coming from. When she finally found the source of the smell, she realized that he had been peeing in the plant on her nightstand. I was laughing so hard that I snorted. I know that may sound cruel but remember what goes around comes around and it may not come how you give it. I did apologize for laughing but I told her, you thought you had a prize. She then apologized to me for everything that she had done to me when he and I were together. I reminded her that I told her that she would apologize to me one day. He was by far my worst relationship, and it made me step back for a while. I wanted to do better and to be honest I didn't know how to accomplish that. I was just in the world trying to figure out how to get the love I desired without all the bad shit to go along with it. There had to be love out there that didn't come with a lot of tears and hurt. I had been hurting long enough and I was not going to stand for that shit anymore. That brings me to this sad and devastating story of thinking you have finally figured this shit out, only to find out that you were sadly mistaken. I was still living in Los Angeles, and I had gone home for the holiday. A few of my friends had come home as well. So, one night we decided we would go wine tasting at this place downtown. While hanging out I saw a guy that I had attempted to date when I lived in Houston before, and it didn't work out. Not because I didn't like him or anything like that. It was because he felt that a woman shouldn't be looking for a relationship, she should just ride the wave. So, I stopped seeing him and moved on. I wanted a relationship not a booty call. When I saw him, he was just as handsome as I had remembered. We locked eyes and smiled at one another. I had not stopped liking him, I just knew my worth, at least I thought I did. He found his way over to me and we spoke while embracing one another. As we talked, he said, "I regret the day I let you go!" I felt my heart flutter because I really liked him and thought he would be the change I had been looking for. So, we decided that we would date long distance. I was in LA, and he was in Houston. We would travel back and forth to see one another until I transferred to New Orleans. I told him that if at any time he found someone else, or this traveling back and forth became too much to let me know. I would rather know than we drag on something that was not going to work. I finally transferred to New Orleans and had been there for a few months. I drove home to Houston for the holiday with my sons, so that we could spend Christmas and New Years with the family. I also had the opportunity to spend time with the man I had fallen in love with. We had an amazing time and then I had to go back to work. I had just gotten back to work and was driving in that particular morning. My phone rang and it was my good friend on the other end asking me if I had been on Facebook that morning. I had not and she suggested that I go and look at my boyfriend's page. I pulled over and went to his page. I started seeing congratulations all down his page and I found it strange because it was his birthday. I continued to scroll, and I finally got to what they had been congratulating him on. He had gotten married! I had just left him that weekend and he had gotten married. I was then hysterically crying on the side of the road, and I was on my way to work. I called him and confronted him about what I had saw and how could he have done that to me. The only words that came out of his mouth were "My bad!" The only thing I could do at that time was hang up the phone and continue my utter devastation of tears and pity on myself. You would be surprised at how you can feel your heart break and all you want to do is make him hurt as much as you hurt. Because the hurt turns into anger shortly after. I'm not sure if you ever get over the anger of it all. I mean eventually you do but I can say that I was angry for quite a while. That same year I went to Houston for All Star weekend to meet up with some friends, go to a few parties and blow off a little steam. Friday night we got dressed really cute and went to an NBA party. As soon as I walk into the party, I see him, and he is the DJ for the event. I hesitated a little, but I was going to stay at this party I spent my money to attend. My friend was like, you want me to go over and push his equipment over? We laughed and I went to the bar. I ordered a shot of tequila I was feeling jumpy. I wanted to stay but I was so angry and seeing him brought it all crashing back on me. After a few drinks I told my friend we had to leave because I didn't want to make a scene and I felt like I would eventually do that. Especially because I was drinking and the more, I drank the worst I felt. Of course, he saw me leave and he sent me a text, don't you think we need to talk? That text angered me even more because when I called you the day, I found out you could give a fuck less about what I needed. Now, you see me, and you want to talk. I replied, yes, I would think we do. He wanted me to meet him somewhere I really can't remember but I knew that I was not going there. If you want to talk to me, it will be on my turf. Needless to say, we never had that conversation. Funny story, the next day I'm at the park doing my traditional 3-mile run whenever I come home to visit. My cell rings and I really don't recognize the phone number but it's Texas so I figure I will know them. It was his wife calling me. She had read the messages in his phone from the night before and wanted to know what was going on. I asked her a simple question, "Are you sure you want to have this conversation with me?" I told her who I was and how we got to the point of where we were! She proceeded to tell me that she knew that he was cheating on her put could not prove it. I told her no, he was cheating on me with you! Then I gave her some advice because I never want to ruin anyone's marriage. I don't care how hurt I am that he married her. I told her to make a decision that day to start from that moment a relationship of communication and try to get to the point of trust. If you hold on to this, it will eat at your marriage, and it won't work. If you want this marriage and you love him then work, it out. I never heard from either of them again. I didn't need to I was done with all of it. I was in New Orleans, and I was ready for a new start and a relationship was the furthest thing from my mind. I hated my boss but loved my job, so I cried a lot. My youngest son was getting into trouble at school, so I was frustrated because I really didn't know what to do to fix it. I put him in counseling hoping that would help but to no avail. I finally said I'm going to take you to your father and see if he can help. He got even worse, so I went and got my child and brought him back home. Still working on me and what I wanted out of life at that time. I turned 40 in New Orleans, and I took myself out to a fancy dinner. I drank good wine and ate good food. It wasn't that I didn't want a man I just wanted to make sure that I got the right man in my life this time. I had to work on me and what that meant to me. I had been doing what I was doing for so long and it was not working. I had to point the finger at myself because I was the common denominator. Whatever the issue was it was in me. As I'm working on me, I'm also working on my youngest son. He was priority number one and I had to make sure I was doing the right things for him while on this journey of fixing me. My oldest son was a great support throughout this entire process. He saw my frustrations and he would give me a hug or tell me it was going to be ok when I needed that. So, one Saturday after dropping the boys off at the Church in my neighborhood where they attended a youth program, I decided to go have me some food and a cocktail. There was a restaurant in Metairie that had the best nachos I had had in a long time. Plus, the margaritas were amazing. I sat at the bar and ordered. While I waited on my food a white couple comes into the restaurant and sat next to me. I mentioned their race only because of the situation that took place. The female next to me struck up a conversation and as we talked, she asked me why a woman as pretty as myself was in there alone. I didn't want to get into the real reason, so I said, "Just moved here and I really don't know anyone" that was a partial truth. So, her boyfriend said, "You single? I have the perfect person for you" as he pulls out his cell phone. I'm cringing because I think he is calling a white person and I was not really into them like that. Now, don't get me wrong, I don't find anything wrong with interracial dating if you're into it. I was not really into it. I hear him talking to the person he called and then he hands me the phone. I start to laugh because I was really nervous about this interaction that was taking place. I say, "Hello" and the voice on the other end replies, "Hello". I'm relieved because he is a black man, there is something in a black man's voice that lets me know they are black. I don't know what he looks like and that is a real problem as well! We chat for a few minutes and exchange phone numbers. Thank God my food came out and I just sat and ate the rest of the time. I left them at the bar and went home, thinking about the encounter I had just had. I had no intentions of calling this person. His name was Raymond, and he was from New Orleans, I could tell that from the accent. It was a week or so later when I got a phone call, and it was him on the other end. Asking how I was doing and other questions to get to know me. I was not interested but I obliged the conversation. I didn't want to come across as rude. Once we finished the niceties, he told me to call him sometime. I said that I would, but I knew that I wasn't. A few more weeks went by and one night he sent me a picture of himself, and he was handsome! So, I sent him a picture of myself. I made sure that the picture was very conservative. He called me after that, and we went on our first date. I was still nervous because sometimes people will send you an old picture of themselves. Our first date was at Copelands, and we talked for hours but I still wasn't really interested. I was working on me, remember? I think a week later we went on our second date, which was a ride on his Harley to the Daiquiri shop for one of my favorite daiquiri's. We again talked for hours, and I made a decision that day that I was going to make him date me. Something I had never done before. I was going to go out on real dates and really get to know one another. There was going to be no sex in that process because that was easy to do, and I wanted something different. I wanted a real sustainable relationship that was not built on how good we were in bed. Of course, everyone wants their partner to be good in bed, but I was going to just hope for the best. I think we went at least three months before we were intimate, and I think that made it even more arousing! Before I knew it, we had been together for one year. The second year flew by as well and our relationship was really effortless. To be honest, I didn't know what I was going to do because I was up for orders, and I was going to PCS to somewhere else. I knew how I felt but I was so used to just getting up and leaving, it had become second nature to me. I received orders to Phoenix, AZ and he was devastated, and I didn't know how to fix it. I told him that we could see one another often by flying back and forth but in my mind, I really didn't think it would work. The day I was to leave I went to say goodbye and that was the day I realized I loved him, and I wanted him in my life. I didn't think it was going to work though. We both cried that day and I left for Phoenix. I got to Phoenix and got myself settled. Working as hard as I could because I was still trying to get promoted. Ray and I talked often and made plans for him to visit. His first visit was great. We did a staycation at this small boutique hotel downtown Phoenix and had an amazing time. At some point we went ring shopping and I tried on at least 12 rings. Starting with the most expensive to the least expensive. The first ring I tried on was the one I wanted, and it was beautiful. I actually tried it on twice. I know the rule about how much a ring should cost but I didn't want to put that kind of pressure on him. Plus, I thought we were just looking for fun. The next visit was that early November. I wanted to go home for the holiday but that would have been very expensive, so I ended up staying in Phoenix. The visit was going great, but I had a hair appointment for that Saturday, and I asked him to attend with me. He knew my hairstylist because I had talked about her so much and I wanted them to meet. When we got there, they hit it off really well and I was impressed that he didn't complain about having to sit and wait for me to get my hair done. After she finished, I told him that since he was so gracious and patient with me getting my hair done that, I was going to treat him to a very nice lunch at Pappadeaux. One of my favorite places to eat. They have great seafood, and the drinks are phenomenal. When we get to the restaurant and are about to be seated, he wanted a specific area to be seated in and I thought that was a little strange, but I was just like ok, that's fine. We sat and the waitress came over to take our order. We ordered oysters as an appetizer, and I really don't remember what my main course was because it was insignificant in comparison. We were chatting and laughing, and I was having a great time. He gave me a little velvet black sack and I took it not really thinking anything. It looked like something that would hold jewelry, so I thought he was showing me his ring that he had gotten repaired because the stone had fallen out of the eye. Now, I really don't know why that thought came to my head but that is what I thought. As I'm opening the sack, I'm really not paying much attention just still holding a conversation with him. I untie the sack and it falls open on the table to reveal a beautiful diamond ring. I realize that it was not the ring I thought it was and as I look up at him, he asked me to marry him. I immediately start to cry and say yes, as he is putting the ring on my finger. It was the ring that I had tried on twice. The ring was absolutely beautiful, and I had just become the happiest women in the world. He had planned this the entire time, and I was oblivious to it all. The reason I was not expecting anything like this was because after I had tried on the rings that day, he called me and said that the ring that I really wanted had been sold so we would have to go out and look again. I immediately called my mother and told her that Ray had asked me to marry him. I will never forget her response. "It's about time, I could not hold on to the secret that much longer." Ray had asked my mother for my hand in marriage months earlier. This man was so amazing, and I was lucky to have had him come into my life. It was time to plan a wedding and I was so excited. We had to put if off for a while because I had gotten promoted to Chief Petty officer and I had to go through the initiation process. So, while I'm getting initiated, I am looking for dresses, venues and flowers for my wedding. The Chief Season was horrible for me, and my stress level was on 10. At the end of the season my fiancé, mother, brother, sister-in-law, niece, my son and one of my closest friends attended my pinning ceremony. My mother who had never gotten on an airplane in her life of 78yrs flew to my pinning and wrote me this amazing letter that I read in front of the audience as I cried. I was so proud of myself. I had done it and my family came to witness this momentous occasion. "To my prestigious daughter, Latonya Yvette Robinson. I want you to know I am so proud of the beautiful and bold young lady you have grown up to be. Not only am I proud of the many accomplishments you have made through this journey of life, but your entire family is proud of you. I have marveled at the many things you have done from high school being a cheerleader to being Ms. Santa Clarita Valley, Ms. New Orleans, and Ms.

Louisiana State. I must say only a mother could be so proud of the things I once dared to do. I knew when you decided to join the Navy you were going to go far. This was just a journey that God bestowed upon you. If I have not said it to you once "you are my rock!" Life for our family has been hard but we have managed to get through the pain. Just know the hard work and dedication I have seen you exert through work and family is greater than I can express. Again, my beautiful daughter you are becoming a Chief in the Navy is just another blessing that God has allowed me to live and enjoy this great honor you deserve." Is what my mother wrote. My heart was full, and I was the happiest I had ever been. I had a man who loved me and put a ring on it and my family and friends in tow. March of 2016, I married the man who loves me more than I could ever imagine a man could. See, I had thought that I could not be loved like that, so I had resolved to being partially loved. That's a love that works when it's good for him. He knows me and everything about me is ok with him. On the day of our wedding, I stood back there thinking I am the luckiest woman I know right now. As my eyes well up with tears, I told myself don't you dare cry and mess up your pretty makeup! You have done it baby girl, you have found the man that at the end of the day, you could not imagine yourself without.

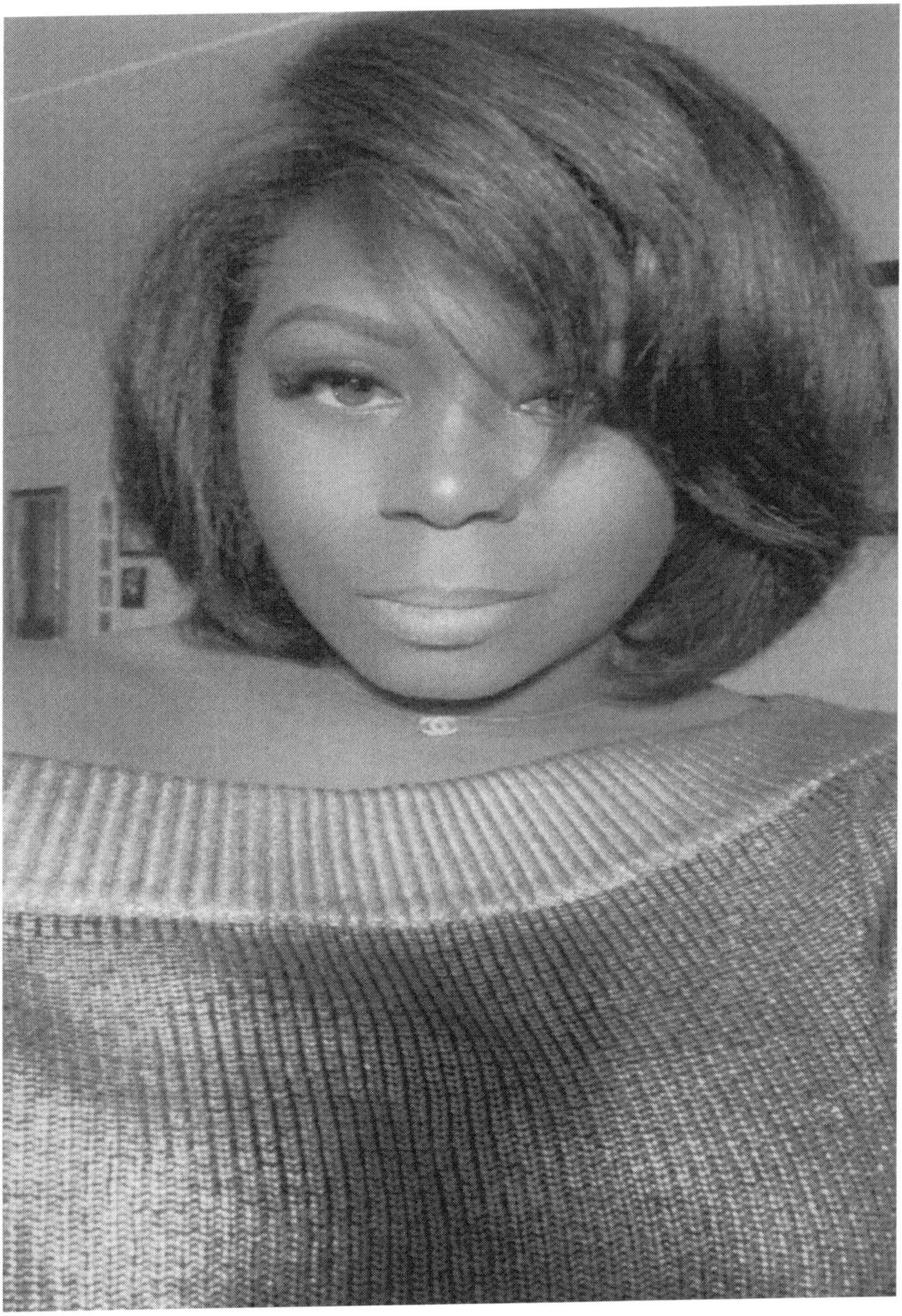

A LETTER TO THE 8 YEAR OLD ME

> *"She overcame everything that was meant to destroy her."*
>
> — Janet Gwen

A LETTER TO THE 8 YEAR OLD ME

Hey you, you have really had a go of it. I just want to say I am so sorry for everything you have went through. I am sorry for the adult me blaming you for being weak and not telling anyone what was happening to you. I am sorry for feeling like you must have done something to make these men do these horrible things to you. I am sorry for a grown ass fucking man finding an 8yr old child attractive. Most of all I am sorry that it took me this long to heal you. Being an 8yr old in a world of adults was probably the most difficult thing you have experienced in your life but guess what, you made it! The reality of it all is you were a child, and you at that time thought like a child, moved like a child, and loved like a child. Loving people are what children do because that's all they want in return. What happens when someone shows you a love that is wrong? It messes up your understanding of love and you live a life thinking that is how you show love. You made no mistakes love, you lived how you were supposed to live, and I want you to never look back at those moments with shame anymore. Unfortunately, all that horror and pain made you what you are today. You didn't know what that would do to your life at that time. You didn't know that it would hinder your self-esteem, your self-worth, your self-love. I held on to you for so many years because I didn't know how to heal you and I felt so bad that you were hurt. I was still hurting. They broke your heart and there was nothing I could do to mend it because I was broken hearted too. You no longer have to sit in the corner anymore looking at me and wondering what's next. Your dreams no longer have to be nightmares. You can sleep and know that the monsters have been slayed and you can heal. Baby girl, every time I saw a little girl that looks to be around your age I would struggle because it would remind me of you and all the sadness, I know you felt, and I would pray that child was not going through the same thing. I want to see a young girl sitting on her father's, grandfather's, uncle's, brother's, and cousin's lap and not cringe. I want to see a man loving on his daughter, granddaughter, niece, sister, and cousin as normal. I want to forgive the men that hurt me and turned my life into a series of fuck shows and what the fucks. I want to love unconditionally and know that it's not considered weak. I want to see me as perfectly imperfect and be completely ok with everything I see. Most of all I want to forgive me for being me! This journey has been hard, and I have so much further to go but I am here and present and I will not stop. I am worthy of this healing and by the way, you are too! To the 8yr old me baby girl you stand relieved, I have the Watch! This journey has been long, but I can tell you it's been so worth it. Every day I have the opportunity to change someone's life and I am so proud of that. When I am in front of young men and women, I can't help but think of you and that motivates me to motivate them to become a greater part of themselves. Every time I look in the audience, I know there is a young person out there that has the same demons that I carried. I try to make my words a comfort place for them to find peace in a world of chaos and pain. It wasn't mine or their fault for the pain we endured. Hopefully, the friction will turn them into a beautifully polished diamond that the world can be in awe of. You have come a long way little girl and I will never let you down again. There are so many people out here who love you and want nothing but the best for you. So, keep going forward because the alternative is not an option. You are that coal that has been bumped, bruised and picked at but from all that damage you became the most flawless diamond. No one could have told me that that damaged eight-year-old would be a wife, mother, Chief Petty Officer in the United States Navy, MS Santa Clarita, MS New Orleans, MS Louisiana State, and last but surely not least MRS Freedom USA Woman. What happened to you was a small bleep in your life and even though it changed you it did not break you. You did your thing beautiful, rare black bird, you did your thang.

Made in the USA
Columbia, SC
16 July 2022